Hurry Up and Meditate

D0064027

Hurry Up and Meditate

*Your Starter Kit for Inner Peace
and Better Health*

David Michie

SNOW LION PUBLICATIONS
ITHACA, NEW YORK

Snow Lion Publications
P. O. Box 6483
Ithaca, NY 14851 USA
(607) 273-8519
www.snowlionpub.com

Designed and typeset by Gopa & Ted2, Inc.
Printed in USA on acid-free recycled paper.

ISBN-10: 1-55939-306-8
ISBN-13: 978-1-55939-306-5

Library of Congress Cataloging-in-Publication Data

Michie, David.
    Hurry up and meditate : your starter kit for inner peace
and better health / David Michie.
        p. cm.
    Includes bibliographical references.
    ISBN-13: 978-1-55939-306-5 (alk. paper)
    ISBN-10: 1-55939-306-8 (alk. paper)
1. Meditation—Buddhism. I. Title.
BQ5612.M53 2008
158.1'2—dc22
                                                2008013927

Contents

Acknowledgments   vii

1 Introduction   1

2 The Physical Benefits of Meditation   15

3 The Psychological Benefits of Meditation   39

4 How to Meditate: The Nuts and Bolts   67

5 Different Types of Meditation   87

6 Seven Ways to Turbocharge Your Meditation   117

7 Measuring Progress   135

8 Using Meditation to Heal   139

9 Troubleshooting   161

10 A Bigger Picture   169

References   177

Further Reading   181

This book is dedicated with heartfelt gratitude to my meditation teachers: Geshe Acharya Thubten Loden, Founder of the Tibetan Buddhist Society, and Les Sheehy, Director of the Tibetan Buddhist Society in Perth, Western Australia, whose kindness I can never repay, and without whom this book could never have been written.

Acknowledgments

~~~~~~

L AST DECEMBER I received an e-mail from some long-standing friends in Scotland. Instead of the Christmas letter and family pictures I was expecting, when I opened up the e-mail it was to discover news of an altogether different kind. Mary, who, like her husband, Grant, was a contemporary of mine, had gone to the doctor in early December suffering from fatigue. Instead of being prescribed a booster to help her through the festive season, within days of blood tests and other examinations she was told that she had inoperable cancer and would be lucky to survive until Christmas.

In the weeks that followed this shocking news, Mary and her family were often in my thoughts. After all, you're not supposed to die in your forties, leaving behind a devastated husband and two young kids. In Mary's case that wasn't all she was leaving behind. A gifted artist and designer, her work was in demand both in the UK and internationally, enriching the lives of many people.

When Mary passed away in January, apart from offering wholly inadequate moral support by e-mail, I'm sure I wasn't the only one among her friends who wondered, How would I react if I was given similar news? What if, perhaps next December, the same thing happened to me?

It was at this point I decided to write *Hurry Up and Meditate*, a book I'd been contemplating for some time, but putting off for no particular reason. Were I to die in twelve months' time, I decided, like Mary, I would rather do so having left behind something which may be valued, even if only by a few people.

So my first heartfelt acknowledgment is to Mary and also to Grant, whose honesty and courage through the whole experience have been quite humbling—and without whom this book may still very well be just an idea in my filing cabinet.

I would also like to offer my sincere thanks to all my fellow meditators who have been so encouraging of my literary efforts. Louise Bladen, Susan Cameron, Richard Ross, Rhonda Sheehan, Cheryl Stedman, and Ineke van Staveren have all been very generous in offering advice, reading typescripts and showing patience at my spectacular inability to distinguish between the two kinds of "practice"—noun vs. verb! My special thanks also to Marg Sheehy, not only for reviewing my work, but also for her tireless management of the many meditation retreats from which I, and my fellow retreatants, have benefited so much.

I am enormously grateful to Elizabeth Weiss, my publisher at Allen & Unwin, who has had such a clear vision for my work from the beginning, and continues to be such a supportive advocate.

Of course, I could never have embarked on this book if it wasn't for my meditation teacher Les Sheehy. Les's wisdom and compassion over many years have helped me cultivate an inner peace and a sense of purpose way beyond anything I could have imagined in early adulthood. I only hope I can pass on a fraction of his inspiration, and in so doing repay some of the debt I owe him.

Lastly, and closest to home, loving thanks to my darling wife, Koala, who has been unwavering in her support of my meditation practice and my constant companion on the roller-coaster ride of life as a writer.

CHAPTER ONE

Introduction

~~~~~~

I KNOW OF NO MORE ENCOURAGING FACT THAN THE UNQUESTIONED
ABILITY OF A MAN TO ELEVATE HIS LIFE BY CONSCIOUS ENDEAVOR.
HENRY DAVID THOREAU

YES, IT'S a deliberately provocative title. After all, being in a hurry is the opposite of meditating, isn't it? If we have a lot going on in our lives, is it realistic trying to find even more time to meditate? The idea of infusing our daily schedule with newfound tranquility may sound appealing—but not everyone is temperamentally suited to sitting around in the lotus position chanting "Om." Not to mention the fact that some of us just have very active minds. We'd like to meditate—but we're simply not capable of switching off.

Whoa! Back up a little! These are what I call the most common "buts" of meditation—as in, "I'd like to meditate, but . . ." And the amazing thing is that it's *exactly* the people who use the "too busy," "too hard," and "too hyper" justifications who stand to gain the most from meditation. How can I be so sure of this? Because I was one of them.

This book has been written for people in a hurry, and its message is quite simple: meditation is probably the best chance you've got to combat stress, cultivate happiness, enhance your performance, realize your goals, and attain mastery of your mental, emotional, and material destiny. Big claims, you may think—but they're supported by compelling evidence.

THE SCIENCE OF MEDITATION

In recent years technology has made it possible to monitor the impacts of mental activity. Measurable, observable, and repeatable studies, conducted by many credible researchers from a wide range of highly respected universities and medical centers, leave no room for doubt about the benefits of meditation. A summary of key studies is provided in Chapters 2 and 3 of this book because they provide the motivation needed to begin and sustain this profoundly life-enhancing practice.

Once you've been meditating for a while, of course, you won't give two hoots about scientific studies because you'll have direct, first-hand experience of how good it feels to meditate—and how stressful it feels not to. Just as we don't need scientific research to persuade us that a long cool drink is wonderful on a hot summer's afternoon, once we've experienced the benefits of meditation on a personal level, the clinical whys and wherefores no longer seem so relevant. Though in the beginning they have an important part to play in getting us motivated—and keeping us that way.

If I were to summarize the scientific evidence in just a couple of paragraphs, it's probably fair to say that if meditation were available in capsule form, it would be the biggest selling drug of all time. Where else can you find a treatment regime which lowers blood pressure and heart rate, providing highly effective anti-stress therapy, without any side effect whatsoever? Which, in addition, not only improves immune function, leading to less chance of catching a cold or flu bug, but which also significantly decreases our likelihood of being struck by a life-threatening illness like cancer or heart disease? Which improves neural coordination and, over time, actually changes the neuroplasticity of our brains, making us more efficient thinkers? Which boosts production of DHEA—the only hormone known to decrease directly with age—thereby slowing the aging process? Which can form a powerful part of any complementary treatment regime for cancer and other illnesses—a function so important I have devoted a whole chapter to this subject. And these are just some of the *physical* benefits.

Turning to matters of the mind, scientists have shown that meditation heightens activity in the left prefrontal cortex of the brain, which is associated with happiness and relaxation, helping minimize use of all those anti-depressants and anti-anxiety drugs which our society consumes in such terrifying quantities. Meditation improves concentration and activates gamma waves—the state of consciousness in which higher-level thinking and insight occurs. It improves our awareness of everything around us, including other people's moods and feelings. It enhances our sense of zest, vitality, and *joie de vivre.*

It's worth mentioning at this early stage that the word "meditation" covers a very wide range of practices and techniques, all of which have their own particular purpose and emphasis. This is explained more fully in Chapter 5, which provides a range of different meditation types to explore.

But all in all, any objective assessment of the effects of meditation, which are so powerful, so positive and so all-pervasive, can reach only one conclusion: if we're not doing so already, we should hurry up and meditate!

Interestingly, the counterpoint to this is also true. If we want to hurry up—if we want to lead productive, fulfilled, well-rounded, and happy lives—meditation is the rocket fuel we need to propel us. Not only can we find the resources to turbo-charge our performance, by cultivating meditation practices we can also begin to discover a new richness and beauty even in the midst of a busy daily schedule. We have the capacity to create a sense of inner peace and objectivity which not only makes life a lot more pleasant, but also helps us work towards our goals more effectively.

A personal story

While the scientifically established benefits of meditation are important, this book isn't only about the empirical evidence emerging from laboratories. I'd also like to share my personal story, and if I come across as a tad evangelical, it's because meditation is a subject close to my heart.

I'm a person in a hurry and I've been meditating for over fourteen years. Starting out as someone who couldn't keep his bum on a cushion for more than a few minutes, I now usually end my one-hour morning meditation sessions wishing I didn't have to stop. My concentration has moved from almost nonexistent to much improved. And when I think of my life-style now versus ten years ago, there's no comparison. Then I was a harassed mid-level executive, with very limited time or capacity to enjoy life. Now I find myself working less, earning more, and able to pursue the interests that fulfill me—such as writing books like this one.

Having said all that, I'm not making any grand claims about my meditation prowess. In many ways meditation is exactly like going to the gym or learning to play a musical instrument. No matter how good you get, there's always plenty of room for improvement. The measure for comparison is not other people, but your own personal baseline.

It's worth emphasizing that to benefit from meditation it's not necessary to begin with hour-long daily sessions, to adopt an austere lifestyle, or to take off to the mountains for month-long retreats. Even a few minutes of spot meditation, practiced regularly, make an immediate and appreciable difference to our everyday well-being.

I should also add that while meditation has been embraced, in different ways, by all the major religious traditions, this book is intended for use by people in a hurry, whether or not you follow a particular religion. The focus of *Hurry Up and Meditate* is not so much on belief systems as on improving mental and physical health. That said, the opportunity to invoke religious symbols may be useful to some readers, and I'll be sure to refer to these opportunities.

For those readers who do follow a religious tradition, and may be anxious about how meditation fits in, I can think of no better advice than that given by Ian Gawler, the inspiring founder of The Gawler Foundation, who survived cancer against all medical expectations, and has gone on to help many thousands of cancer patients do the same: "While some people are apprehensive that meditation may conflict with their beliefs, the usual experience is that it leads to a heightened appreciation of their particular religious leanings and a greater level of personal joy."

As a Tibetan Buddhist, I will draw on the rich meditative heritage of my own tradition. While *Hurry Up and Meditate* is not about Buddhism, it is my heartfelt wish that readers of my previous work, *Buddhism for Busy People*, will find in this book all the detail and understanding they need to make meditation the same profoundly life-enhancing practice that it has become for me.

Coming home

Just as golfers try to improve their handicaps and classical musicians work through their exam levels, meditators have a nine-level yardstick by which to measure their progress. It's important to mention this early on, to correct the mistaken impression some people have that meditation is some kind of undirected, touchy-feely, "Hey man, you've just gotta, like, bliss out" activity.

On the contrary, meditation prescribes rigorous methodologies which have been practiced for well over two and a half thousand years. It involves discipline and hard work—and there's a chance that at some point you may get so frustrated you'll consider throwing in the towel.

But if you've been meditating properly, even for only a few months, you won't be able to. At some point, perhaps with a sigh of resignation, you will once again resume your place on the meditation cushion because you'll have discovered that meditation is the best way you know of coming home. This has certainly been my experience. And I know there is nothing very unusual about my journey so far. Speaking to other meditators, as I frequently do, it's clear that while we all share the same challenges, we also experience the same life-changing benefits.

Ask a group of meditators why they started their practice and you'll get a variety of answers. These won't be expressed in scientific terms—I have never met anyone who said they meditated to improve their neuroplasticity. Instead you'll hear about the benefits of meditation from a more subjective perspective.

Some people begin with a very specific intention: to support a battle against cancer or some other serious medical condition. To help restore a sense of calm after having been through a stressful life event, such as relationship or career trauma. As an aid to learning, particularly in preparing for important exams. And there's no question that meditation can be an extremely powerful tool in all these cases.

But whatever the original starting point, it's often the case that people discover benefits way beyond what they originally signed up for. Yes, meditation helps us get a grip on problems where they originate—in our minds—but it offers us far more than merely removing the negatives from our lives.

WHAT EXACTLY IS GOOD MENTAL HEALTH?

In the same way that someone free from any diagnosable illness is not necessarily brimming with good health, just because we don't suffer from depression or stress doesn't mean we're in especially good mental shape. Just as we need to apply some effort to keep physically fit, keeping mentally trim, taut, and terrific is something we've got to work on. And arguably the best of all starting points is meditation.

What do I mean by being in good mental shape? A greater feeling of happiness is the most obvious benefit which keeps meditators coming back for more. A sense of deep-down inner peace and resilience, improving one's ability to weather the inevitable storms of life. Enhanced concentration, enabling rapid processing of work and other tasks. A more outward-looking, panoramic perspective, providing the basis for greater equanimity in our dealings with others.

Whatever we wish to achieve in life, whatever our chosen path to self-fulfillment, meditation provides us with an extremely powerful tool, because through its practice we become more coherent, integrated, and purposeful at all levels of behavior. And if we still don't know what our path to self-fulfillment might be, meditation may help us find it.

Finding peace in the eye of the storm

Beneath the teasing title of this book is the suggestion of a much bigger question. As people in a hurry, is it also possible to lead a contemplative life? Can work deadlines, mortgage repayments, and complicated family and personal relationships combine with meditation and inner growth? Is it possible to find peace in the eye of the storm? Of course, you already know what my response to those questions will be, so let me back it up with an explanation.

Among the most commonly prescribed, but still rapidly growing, drugs in the Western world are various classes of psychiatric drugs, be they antidepressant, antianxiety, stress management, uppers or downers by whatever name. In the UK, over thirteen million prescriptions for antidepressants are issued every year to an estimated 3.5 million patients. In the US over eight million people are using antidepressants, and even in Australia, which has an international reputation for sunny optimism, depression is now the fourth most common reason that people see the doctor.

So pervasive are psychiatric, not to mention nonprescribed, drugs that most of us either have used them ourselves or know people who do. But the amazing thing is that when people take their daily antidepressant or draw on their recreational joint, they do so without any expectation that it will result in a change to their external circumstances. Taking a Prozac is not a known cause for large and unexplained credits to appear in one's bank account, or for one's irksome boss to undergo a personality transplant. But users *do* expect to feel better about things. Implicit in the act of taking such medication is the acceptance that even if "reality" doesn't change, we can still feel a whole lot better about it by changing our mood, our pharmacological make-up, our interpretation of what is going on around us.

Which is exactly what meditation does—except without the toxic side effects. No one is disputing that even the most mentally robust among us may at some point in our lives benefit from pharmacological support. But for most of us, most of the time, why pump our bodies with mind-altering chemicals if we can get the same result, and a whole lot more benefits besides, through natural means? The most powerful pharmaceutical manufacturer is to be found not in the industrial sites outside our capital cities, but between our ears. Why not take control of our own built-in pharmacy to relieve stress, elevate mood, and help manage illness?[1]

So, to answer the question about whether or not we can combine tranquil contemplation with a helter-skelter lifestyle, the answer is not so much "we can" as "we must." If we're leading frenetic lives, burning the candle at both ends, this is exactly *why* we need to cultivate inner calm. If others around us are agitated and stressed out, that's precisely the reason we need to be more relaxed, positive, and benevolent. We may not always be able to change the world around us, but we can definitely change our attitude towards it.

At a deeper level it is perhaps worth asking why, both collectively and individually, we feel the need to keep so busy, and why we so quickly become bored and lonely when we're stripped of all the busyness and distraction with which we fill our lives. Nineteenth-century American poet Ralph Waldo

1 Some people experiencing mood swings and milder forms of depression may be able to use meditation in place of medication. However, for people with a serious mental illness it is strongly recommended that you consult your doctor before starting meditation. With some conditions it may not be possible to stop taking medication, but meditation can be a very helpful additional support.

Emerson wrote amusingly about the wish to escape from one's self: "I pack my trunk, embrace my friends, embark on the sea, and at last wake up in Naples, and there beside me is the Stern Fact, the Sad Self, unrelenting, identical, that I fled from."

Are the circumstances of our lives that keep us so busy created entirely by others, or should we take some responsibility for them? What is it that makes us want to avoid a more simple, unhurried life—and can meditation provide the key?

IMPRISONMENT OR FREEDOM?

A Buddhist monk I know used to hold regular meditation classes for prisoners. Over the years he got to know some of them quite well. Once he was asked by a group of lifers to describe a typical day in the monastery. Belonging to the austere Theravadan tradition, he explained how everyone had to get up at four o'clock in the morning for the first meditation session of the day, followed by more study and meditation classes throughout the morning. Lunch, the main meal, was eaten out of a single bowl—main course and any donated dessert all off the same plate—before the afternoon was spent doing manual work on the monastery property. There was no supper, just a cup of tea, and in the evening there was more study and meditation, which only ended around 10:00 p.m.

There was, of course, a ban on sex, alcohol, drugs, TV, newspapers, magazines, and similar distractions. No money or personal possessions were allowed. Compared to prison, the regime he described was so harsh that one of the prisoners couldn't contain himself: "You could always come and live here with us!" he burst out in spontaneous sympathy, before realizing what he was saying.

After the ensuing laughter had subsided, the monk couldn't help reflecting on the paradox. His monastery with its strongly ascetic regime had a long waiting list of people who wanted to join as novices. And yet everyone in the very much more comfortable jail couldn't wait to get out.

In other words, it's not our circumstances so much as our feelings, beliefs, and attitudes about those circumstances that make us happy or otherwise. Have we arrived at our current lifestyle through freedom of choice? Or do we feel imprisoned in jobs or relationships from which we long to escape? Is our daily life an authentic reflection of our interests and values? Or merely a series of burdens and responsibilities from which we wish we could break free?

You may be wondering how meditation can help in any of this. Well, to quote the well-worn business adage, you can't manage what you don't monitor. If we don't keep regular track of our income and expenditures, how can we possibly stay on top of our personal or company finances? If our goal is to lose weight and we don't monitor how much we eat and how much we exercise, how can we be sure that calories out exceed calories in?

In the same way, changing our interpretations of the world requires us to be aware of what our current interpretations are. Meditation provides a direct support by helping us develop improved levels of mindfulness of our thoughts. By identifying our current mental habits we can start to replace ingrained negative mental patterns with more positive ones.

Even a small improvement in mindfulness can help create very important change. Little by little we can turn our prisons into monasteries.

MASTERS OF OUR OWN REALITY

UNDERSTANDING OF PROCESS ENABLES A PERSON TO GAIN CONTROL OF THAT PROCESS OR TO GAIN FREEDOM FROM BEING CONTROLLED BY IT.

THE DALAI LAMA

As technological advancements enable neurologists to study the workings of the mind in greater detail, we are seeing a wonderful convergence take place. Ancient meditation-based wisdom and contemporary science are drawing together. We are coming to understand that our sensory awareness—such as sight—has as much to do with mental functioning and the way we interpret stimuli as with our sense receptors. We are gaining new insights showing how pleasure or pain is as much a result of our conditioning as our circumstances. Very recent studies confirm that we have it in our power to cultivate positive states of mind, and even change our neural pathways to enjoy happiness on a more ongoing basis. In short, contemporary research is affirming the ancient wisdom that we are the creators of our own reality.

If we don't like the way we feel, we have the power to change it. We don't have to wait to be rescued by a shift in external circumstance. Whether we are aware of it or not, we are the shapers of everything we are experiencing today, the coauthors of our mental continuum way into the future.

Which presents us with a simple choice. We can focus all our efforts on trying to manage an external reality in the hope that our deepest wishes are realized, our lives fulfilled, and we will never have to face any serious hardship (yeah, right!). Or we can take charge of our own mental destiny. It's no simple choice because the meditative path is not an easy one. But how often are great things accomplished without effort?

More important is the knowledge that with perseverance, an open heart, and clarity of purpose we can achieve profound inner transformation. If we choose, we can change our experience of reality so that our happiness is less conditioned on the quirks of circumstance, and instead becomes an abiding presence. We can replace our short-term concerns with a more panoramic sense of destiny beyond anything we might currently imagine. We can celebrate a more transcendent understanding of who we are and why we're here. To begin, all we need is a small cushion, a quiet room—and a strong sense of adventure!

CHAPTER TWO

The Physical Benefits of Meditation

THE GREATEST REVOLUTION IN OUR GENERATION IS THE DISCOVERY
THAT HUMAN BEINGS BY CHANGING THE INNER ATTITUDES OF THEIR
MINDS CAN CHANGE THE OUTER ASPECTS OF THEIR LIVES.

WILLIAM JAMES

I F YOU'RE anything like I was, you'll be reading this book from the point of view of a skeptic. Someone who has yet to make up his or her mind about meditation, perhaps. But one way or another you'll be looking for facts, hard evidence, before investing any of your precious time in what may seem a decidedly left-field activity.

As it happens, there's a significant and ongoing flow of data from a wide variety of institutions confirming the physical benefits of meditation. So much so that when researching for this book, as well as collating some of the mainstream research I was already familiar with, I was surprised by the sheer volume and variety of studies, many of them conducted only recently.

Researchers Michael Murphy and Steven Donovan have compiled a comprehensive work, *The Physical and Psychological Effects of Meditation*, which summarizes the findings of literally hundreds of research studies. They suggest that the physiology of meditation has received attention out of all proportion to other meditation benefits because for many scientists "what is immediately physical and material constitutes all there is to reality."

We'll explore other elements of reality in following chapters. But for the moment, let's focus on the physical, and the wealth of evidence showing that meditation is effective not only in managing stress and preventing heart disease, but also in boosting the immune system, even to the extent of helping combat different forms of cancer. One area that particularly catches my imagination is that of aging: meditation has been shown to lower biological age.

But before we even get to these amazing findings, perhaps we first need to deal with more fundamental questions—like what is the connection between body and mind? Can our thoughts really affect our physiological activity? Very simply, how does meditation work?

THE CONNECTION BETWEEN BODY AND MIND

Most of us have an oddly inconsistent view about the relationship between our bodies and minds as we go about our daily lives. Our usual tendency is to regard our bodies and minds as separate entities, with the former the irksomely unreliable servants of the latter. "I wanted to have a really good workout at the gym, but my legs gave up on me," we might say. Or, "My arm was grazed in a couple of places, but I'm okay."

We have quite a strong sense of mind as the owner or controller of our body. Mind who is disappointed by body's inability to handle a gym workout or quite independent of the bumps and bruises suffered by body.

But then, without even noticing our own inconsistency, we'll also say things like, "When she heard the news she was so shocked her face went white." Or, "He had really bad flu and was feeling depressed."

Now, paradoxically, we assume that mind and body form a systemic whole. We are saying that a mental experience, like hearing bad news, has resulted in bodily change—a white face—or that a physical experience, bad flu, has impacted on a state of mind.

In the past, conventional Western medicine has reinforced the dualistic view of body and mind, with its frequent focus on curing individual, physical symptoms in isolation, without reference to the bigger picture. Murphy and Donovan note that "for three hundred years, the dualism of Descartes has required an absolute separation of mind and body." No doubt the pressures of delivering healthcare, especially in public health systems, is part of the reason that many doctors have little time to respond to anything other than a patient's immediate symptoms, with the emphasis on getting that patient out of the consulting room as fast as possible, prescription in hand, to make time for the next one.

By contrast, Eastern medical traditions originating in India and China view body and mind as a holistic system that needs to be kept in balance. A great deal of consulting time is spent not only on physical diagnosis, but also asking questions about a patient's lifestyle and psychological state of mind. The emphasis is much more all-embracing and preventative.

This is not, by the way, intended as some sort of negative judgment of Western medicine, which clearly has many more sophisticated and powerful methods of treating disease. It is simply to point out a limitation which, fortunately, is being increasingly recognized, because in recent years we have seen Western healthcare move towards a more holistic view. By combining a holistic and preventative approach, which aims to achieve internal balance, with highly effective intervention when necessary, perhaps we are making our way towards a more coherent and integrated understanding of what it means to be healthy.

Many doctors are beginning to suggest stress management or meditation classes instead of only prescribing tranquilizers or sleeping pills. Health insurers are creating policies that cover naturopathy, acupuncture, and traditional Chinese medicine. And more and more Western universities are recognizing the importance of studying the body–mind continuum by setting up dedicated centers, such as the Mind/Body Medical Institute at Harvard University, the Center for Mindfulness in Medicine at the University of Massachusetts, and the Laboratory for Affective Neuroscience at the University of Wisconsin.

THE HOLISTIC REALITY

IF THE MIND IS TRANQUIL AND OCCUPIED WITH POSITIVE THOUGHTS,
THE BODY WILL NOT EASILY FALL PREY TO DISEASE.
THE DALAI LAMA

In reality, we cannot properly account for disease of the body without also understanding dis-ease of the mind. Mind is wired into body. Body is an extension of mind. Even the most subtle changes in one part of the continuum cannot but affect the other. In a way this is so obvious that we take it for granted.

Each of us has, at one time or another, experienced blushing, goose bumps, clammy hands, or a dry mouth—physiological changes which have come about purely because of the content of our thoughts.

Perhaps the most telling of all examples of the body–mind continuum is sexual arousal. Here the response of the body to a particular set of thoughts is amply evident, albeit in men more visibly than women! What further evidence do we need of the direct impact of thoughts on the body? If our minds were unable to create immediate, significant, and complex changes in our bodies, then none of us, quite simply, would exist.

It's not only in times of high emotion or arousal that our bodies respond to our minds, even though these may be the moments at which we most notice the connection. Just as an aircraft autopilot is constantly monitoring, adjusting, and communicating with the navigation, fuel, hydraulic, and other on-board systems, so too our central nervous system provides the "neural network" by which mind and body are in continuous communication, almost all the time at a subconscious level.

Once we accept that body and mind form a systemic whole, the idea of focusing all our attention on only one part of the system—the body—while excluding the other—the mind—seems more than just a little bit crazy. And yet this is what most of us in a hurry do most of the time. We'll take beta blockers to deal with blood pressure, while following the same frenetic schedule, as though what's happening to us is a temporary inconvenience rather than an amber alert that our whole system is out of kilter. We'll try powerful painkilling drugs with harmful side effects to deal with chronic headaches, while the idea of dealing with the source of the problem—an overly stressful lifestyle—doesn't even occur to us.

But what happens when we do take a more holistic approach? When we shift our paradigm so that instead of regarding our bodies as independent of mind, we see them for what they are—as manifestations of the way we think? At this point a whole new dimension opens up to us, together with possibilities that not only offer compelling physical benefits, but also propel us along a path of personal transformation. Following are the powerful, and proven, physical impacts of meditation.

1. Highly effective stress management

The most obvious physical change that occurs when we bring body and mind together in meditation is that breathing naturally slows and, with it, the heartbeat. Blood pressure decreases and so too the metabolic rate. Muscular tension reduces significantly.

In short, we relax.

It's important to note that these physiological changes do not arise merely by resting. Repeated research shows that we can't get the same benefits simply by sitting down and daydreaming or enjoying a cup of tea. In a state of ordinary physical rest, when we make no effort to manage our mental focus, we do not see a lowered rate of metabolism, a decrease in the use of oxygen, or reduced output of carbon dioxide. Nor do we see the heart rate decrease, as it does in meditation, by several beats a minute—in some cases, by as many as fifteen.

When we meditate the lactate concentration in our blood

also decreases by up to a third. Why should this matter? Because blood lactate level is associated with tension and high blood pressure, and the infusion of lactate in the blood produces symptoms of anxiety. Studies have shown a reduction in lactate concentration in meditators of about four times as much as people who are merely resting. A quite separate biological marker of stress—resistance of skin to a mild electric current—has similarly been shown to decline by about four times among meditators.

A different significant effect of meditation is its impact on the hormones released by our bodies. Chocolate, sex, morphine, and acupuncture all stimulate the production of endorphins by our bodies. Joggers and gym junkies are familiar with the postworkout high—nature's way of saying, "keep doing that." So too, meditation increases endorphin output, and the resulting feel-good emotions are only part of the systemic benefits endorphins deliver. In short, meditation not only helps us get rid of unwanted symptoms of stress, it also creates positive body–mind states.

For more than thirty-five years, Dr. Herbert Benson, President of the Mind/Body Medical Institute and Associate Professor of Medicine at Harvard Medical School, has been studying what he calls "the relaxation response," the state elicited by meditation. And as his research has importantly shown, the relaxation response has impacts which go well beyond any specific meditation session. What's more, practicing meditation over a period of time has significant cumulative benefits.

Just as regular gym-goers experience the benefits of their exertions even when they are no longer at the gym—being able, for example, to hurry up a flight of stairs without getting breathless, or effortlessly to carry heavy luggage or grocery bags—so too meditators experience the benefits of their practice when off the meditation cushion. Apart from feeling calmer and better able to deal with the psychological stairs and interpersonal heavy luggage in everyday life, meditators experience benefits that can be measured physiologically. To quote Benson: "Repeated activation of the relaxation response can reverse sustained problems in the body and mend the internal wear and tear brought on by stress."

Like a lot of people, the reason I started to meditate was in an effort to counteract stress. In my early thirties I had a demanding job in one of London's most successful corporate public relations agencies. Having been brought up under the vast blue skies and in the wide open spaces of Africa, it was a tough adjustment for me to live in a shoebox-sized flat, deal with crowded commutes into central London, manage the stresses and long hours demanded of an up-and-coming spin doctor, and then try to find time for a social life. From a career point of view I knew I was in the right place, because I loved the stimulation of working with bright, personable people, being able to work with both language and finance, which have always fascinated me, and feeling at the heart of London's corporate and social whirl. But I felt stressed out. So much so that I actually began breaking out in rashes.

At first I had no idea what was causing the itchy pink dots which would appear on my wrists and ankles for no apparent reason at random intervals during the day. The public health sector doctor to whom I eventually turned told me I was suffering from an allergic reaction, prescribed an antihistamine, and sent me on my way.

It was a naturopath whose flyer hit my doormat at just the right moment who fully explained my situation. Apprehensive about carrying a bottle of antihistamines around in my pocket for an indeterminate period, I made an appointment with this no-nonsense lady, who peered long and hard into my irises, made disapproving clucking sounds, and started asking about my daily routine. Among her questions was: How many cups of coffee did I drink? To which the answer was: Eight.

It turns out that a caffeine intolerance was the cause of the rashes—after I replaced coffee with water for a while, they disappeared completely. But quite apart from that, the naturopath told me that my whole system was stressed. I needed to do something to restore a sense of balance. She suggested meditation.

I'll never forget the intense self-consciousness I felt those first few weeks when I got out of bed ten minutes earlier than usual to meditate. What I was doing felt contrived and artificial. Who the hell did I think I was sitting cross-legged like Maharishi Yogi, supposedly focusing on my breathing, but in reality distracted by every early-morning jet coming down into Heathrow, the sounds of the trash collectors and street sweepers, the angry hooting of horns as early-morning commuters got off to a bad start?

Despite my extremely poor concentration, however, I persisted. Not only because I knew it was supposed to do me good, but also because those ten minutes of being awake and alert were among the precious few when I felt no demands were being put on me. I'd given myself permission *not* to think about all the usual preoccupations—I had the other twenty-three hours and fifty minutes to do that. This was my ten minutes of "time off."

And within even a few weeks I sensed a strange thing happening. At odd moments during the day I would remember that I'd meditated that morning, and in that moment of recollection I'd feel some of the same relaxation and letting go that I had in the morning. What Dr. Benson describes as "the relaxation response" felt, on a subjective basis, a bit like letting the steam out of a pressure cooker. Yes, I still got stressed out, pissed off, and agitated, but for the first time I had resources with which to deal with it. Interestingly, I was also becoming more aware of my moods as they were happening to me, rather than after the event. Without consciously setting out to, even those few minutes of very low-grade meditation were helping me become more aware of how I was feeling and acting during the day, and more conscious that I did have some choice in the matter.

Meditation should come with a health warning: Beware, this practice is addictive! Because even though I was often a reluctant meditator, and despite the struggle I experienced trying to sustain concentration for more than a few moments, the simple fact was that I liked what meditating was doing for me. Yes, it was definitely helping me with my stress. But that was only the beginning. It seemed to be triggering other unexpected changes and insights besides. After a few months, I decided to throw caution to the wind and increase my ten minutes to fifteen!

2. SIGNIFICANTLY LOWERED BLOOD PRESSURE AND
THE COMBATING OF HEART DISEASE

Heart disease is a problem all of us should take seriously. It is by far the biggest cause of death in the developed world; in Australia 27 percent of deaths are caused by heart attacks or strokes, while this figure rises to 33 percent for the UK and a spectacular 39 percent for the US. The causes of cardiovascular or cerebrovascular illnesses can be complex, are sometimes associated with old age, and may have a genetic factor. But the simple truth is that in many cases cardiovascular disease or stroke can be prevented. In particular, if we respond effectively to the common precursor to these illnesses—high blood pressure—we can significantly improve our chances.

When our bodies are under stress, they react in the opposite way to the relaxation response already described. Our blood vessels narrow, our hearts have to work harder, and our blood pressure shoots up. When this happens over a prolonged period of time without respite, it should come as no surprise when our cardiovascular system malfunctions, or breaks down completely—part of the "wear and tear brought on by stress."

Murphy and Donovan have identified more than nineteen research studies which show that meditation lowers blood pressure in people who have "normal" or "moderate" hypertension (high blood pressure). Typically these studies divide subjects into groups, one of which receives meditation training, while a control group undertakes relaxation exercises or something similar. Despite the calming effects you'd expect relaxation exercises would have, they don't show nearly the same level of effectiveness at reducing blood pressure as meditation, which can reduce systolic (peak) readings by as much as 25 mmHg or more (i.e., approximately 20 percent).

To give an example of the kinds of studies undertaken, one clinical trial took 103 patients suffering from coronary heart disease, and over a sixteen-week period showed that the group which practiced meditation did much better than a control sample who simply received education about their condition. Their blood pressure had reduced by 3.4 mmHg (systolic) at the end of the trial compared with an *increase* of 2.8 mmHg for the health education (control) group.

The research, conducted by the Division of Cardiology at the Cedars-Sinai Medical Center, using Transcendental Meditation, a mantra-based meditation method, showed that patients who practiced meditation not only had lower blood pressure readings, but also enjoyed improved insulin resistance and less heart rate variability than the control sample. Another trial showed that heart disease patients who practiced meditation for eight months showed significant improvement (14.7 percent) in exercise tolerance, including at maximal workload, and a significant improvement in ECG readings.

I find it intriguing that meditation, which most of us perceive as an essentially sedentary practice, can actually make us more physically robust. The interplay of mind and body in the development of our muscles and motor skills is a fascinating area of research.

Quite apart from promoting cardiovascular fitness, meditation has also been shown to slow down the impact of arteriosclerosis, or hardening of the arteries. A study among elderly subjects confirmed the reduction of lipid peroxides in the blood by 15 percent among a group practicing meditation versus a control sample—it is lipid peroxides which harden the walls of blood vessels. Supporting this finding is the research by Dr. Herbert Benson showing that the raised levels of nitric oxide we produce when meditating have the effect of dilating the arteries and allowing increased blood flow through the body.

One particularly compelling aspect about many of these studies is the success of meditation even among people who are novice meditators. We are not talking about measuring the physiology of long-practicing Tibetan lamas, or Hindu yogis who have devoted decades to perfecting their concentration. Instead, these are ordinary people, the David Michies of this world, who have only received basic meditation training, but who have nonetheless shown significant and positive responses. What's more, in many cases the people taking part in the studies were only monitored for the short period that the study was under way—weeks or months. While it's encouraging that meditation can have such positive effects, even in the short term among novice meditators, what about the longer term impacts?

It was in an attempt to answer just this question that a researcher from the University of California at Los Angeles, Dr. Robert Keith Wallace, and other researchers measured systolic blood pressure readings among 112 people who regularly practiced meditation. He found that they had an average systolic blood pressure that was 13.7 mmHg to 24.5 mmHg less than the population average. In addition, meditators with more than five years of experience had a mean systolic blood pressure 7.5 mmHg lower than meditators with less experience than this (*Psychosomatic Medicine*, 1983).

The initial positive effects of meditation are therefore only the beginning of the story. Those who choose to stay with the practice can expect even more significant benefits as their meditative experience deepens.

On a personal basis, I can't speak for the cumulative benefits of meditation in terms of managing high blood pressure or heart disease, neither of which has been a problem for me. But it is certainly my experience that the longer I've practiced meditation, over a period of months and years, the more profound and transformational the benefits have been.

3. Boosting our immune systems

We have already noted that during meditation the brain produces higher levels of endorphins, or "feel-good" hormones. There are three major types of endorphins: beta endorphins, found mainly in the pituitary gland; enkephalins; and dynorphins, distributed throughout the nervous system. Quite apart from the feel-good factor, for which endorphins are best known, more importantly they play a part in our immune systems, fighting the war against foreign organisms at a cellular level. In particular, they stimulate the production of natural killer cells, which detect and destroy harmful bacteria and viruses.

When our body–mind systems are stressed, research shows that our output of hormones is cut back, making us more vulnerable to whatever viruses are doing the rounds. Most of us have had direct, personal experience of coming down with flu after a stressful or difficult time at work or home. While we may be aware that a nasty virus is sweeping through our community, whether we catch that virus has more to do with the state of our own defenses than the likelihood that it's a particularly lethal superbug. By contrast, a more relaxed and balanced body–mind system is also a healthy system, generating the hormones needed for our body's self-defense.

Endorphins are not the only hormones known to be stimulated by meditation. The Center for Mindfulness in Medicine at the University of Massachusetts has shown that output of melatonin also increases. Among many other things, melatonin acts as a powerful antioxidant, destroying harmful free radicals which cause such destruction at a cellular level.

DHEA (dehydroepiandrosterone) is another powerful hormone that has been shown, in studies conducted as early as 1968, to increase with regular meditation. DHEA has been long established as a key to boosting the immune function. A number of studies have confirmed its usefulness in combating bacterial, parasitic, and viral infections, including HIV.

In summary, the effects of meditation go well beyond the most visible and tangible benefits of bringing down blood pressure and helping us relax. At a more profound level, meditation creates significant hormonal changes which alter the biochemical balance of our bodies.

My own personal experience of the immune response is emphatically in accord with the research that scientists report. During my premeditation years I used to suffer from a bad flu nearly every winter. The cycle was always wearyingly familiar. It would start with a sore throat, rapidly worsening, soon joined by nasal congestion and a variety of aches and pains, before heading for the full, bedridden whole nine yards: headache, fever, running nose, and coughing. From go to whoa the whole process was rarely less than seven days, and it frequently lasted much longer, leaving me feeling like I'd been run over by the proverbial truck.

Since I started meditating, however, I've experienced far less flu, and when I do pick up bugs I feel a lot less under assault than I used to. I can't remember the last really bad flu I experienced, certainly not one that forced me to bed—it would have been many winters ago.

Interestingly, I was recently talking to a former colleague I hadn't seen for some years when she asked, "Are you still suffering from those terrible headaches? You used to get them quite often." Her query took me by surprise because I'd forgotten I had suffered from headaches. It's as though during that high-stress time, and before I started practicing meditation, I was a different person: recognizably on the same mental and physical continuum, of course, but more prone to infection and generally less robust.

Which is not to say I'm holding up meditation as some kind of global panacea about to put all the major pharmaceutical companies out of business. But on both a clinical and a subjective basis the evidence is there to show the wide-ranging beneficial impacts of bringing mind and body together in harmony. And these impacts may be much greater than what has been scientifically validated so far.

4. BUILDING OUR DEFENSES AGAINST CANCER

Melatonin, produced by the pineal gland in the brain, as well as other parts of the body, is important in the regulation of many hormones in the body, and is possibly best known for its role in controlling circadian rhythm—helping our bodies keep in sync with our minds about deciding when to go to sleep and when to wake up. Several people I know swear by melatonin when taking long-haul flights, and in fact studies have found that melatonin supplements do help prevent jet lag, especially when an individual is crossing five or more time zones.

However, the Center for Mindfulness research, establishing that meditation boosts melatonin output, has implications way beyond helping the sleepless. Melatonin has also been shown in lab studies to stimulate cells called "osteoblasts" that promote bone growth. Given that low melatonin levels are often found in older people, particularly women, boosting these levels could significantly prevent the onset of osteoporosis.

Lower-than-average melatonin levels are also found in women with breast cancer and men with prostate cancer. In both cases, laboratory experiments have found that lower levels of melatonin stimulate the growth of certain types of cancer cells, while adding melatonin inhibits their growth.

Initial, small-scale studies have also shown that, used in conjunction with chemotherapy, melatonin improved the impact of conventional treatment of breast cancer as well as the survival rates in nine out of fourteen patients with metastatic (cancer that has spread to secondary sites in the body) prostate cancer. As the University of Maryland Medical Center notes,

"Interestingly meditation appears to be a valuable addition to the treatment of prostate cancer. The positive effects of meditation may be due to a rise in levels of melatonin in the body. Although these early results are intriguing, more research is needed."

While we have no definitive evidence right now that meditation helps prevent breast and prostate cancer, we do know two things: that meditation boosts melatonin production, and that people with breast and prostate cancer have lower melatonin levels. Until such time as further clinical work is completed, we can't formally connect the dots—but the dots are there.

In this section we have touched on the impact of meditation on healing—one of the key reasons that many people come to meditation to begin with. This is such an important subject that I've devoted an entire chapter to it (see Chapter 8). However, this chapter is focused more on how meditation promotes robust good health and helps prevent illness. And there can be no more powerful way to do this than to slow down the very process that presents us with the most daunting challenges to both our physical and mental well-being: aging.

5. Slowing the rate at which we age

Of all the evidence provided for the physical benefits of meditation, the idea that it can slow down aging may seem the most spectacular—but the clinical results show exactly this. At the heart of this particular miracle is the hormone DHEA. DHEA is the most abundant steroid in the body and the only known hormone that decreases directly with age. In direct, inverse proportion to plummeting DHEA levels, the problems of aging, across a wide variety of fronts, dramatically increase.

While research is still under way to understand the complex mechanisms of DHEA, it may be helpful—even inspirational—to summarize the established benefits which the hormone provides:

- DHEA protects us from heart disease. Research has shown there is a direct relationship between an individual's DHEA levels and their likelihood of developing heart disease.
- DHEA helps fight bacteria and viruses of all kinds, playing an essential role as part of the body's antioxidant and antiviral defenses.
- DHEA has powerful anti-inflammatory properties, lowering the levels of chemical messengers that escalate the inflammatory process, in particular two such messengers called IL-6 and TNF. Chronic inflammation is known to play a critical role in the development of many diseases of aging, including heart disease, rheumatoid arthritis, arteriosclerosis, osteoporosis, and certain cancers.
- Given its potent anti-inflammatory properties, DHEA also has the potential to help HIV patients prevent progression of their condition to full-blown AIDS.
- DHEA helps prevent depression, and controls the harmful effects of excess cortisol found in depressed patients.
- Victims of Alzheimer's disease as well as dementia have been found to have lower DHEA levels than the healthy elderly, underlining the importance of this hormone in brain protection.

- DHEA helps prevent the progressive atrophy of the thymus, which programs cell death and is considered a key driver of aging. Keeping the thymus active is therefore critical to healthy aging.

Exactly why our DHEA levels decline with age is not yet fully understood. Is the decline a function of aging, or a cause of it? But this uncertainty in no way detracts from the simple fact that the longer we maintain higher DHEA levels, the longer we put off the many problems that accompany old age. And the practice of meditation achieves exactly this.

As long ago as 1982 Dr. Robert Keith Wallace published his ground-breaking research on the impact of meditation on aging in the *International Journal of Neuroscience*. Wallace found that among subjects with an average chronological age of fifty years, those who had been practicing Transcendental Meditation for over five years had a biological age twelve years younger than their chronological age. In other words, a fifty-five-year-old meditator had the physiology of a forty-three year old. So marked was the benefit of meditation when practiced regularly over the longer term that some of the subjects in Wallace's study had a biological age an astonishing twenty-seven years younger than their chronological age.

Turning specifically to the effects of meditation on DHEA, different research matched 326 adult meditators with 972 age- and gender-matched controls. That study found significantly higher levels of DHEA among the meditators, with the most marked differences in the oldest age categories. Meditation stimulated increased production of DHEA, especially among those people who most needed it.

A variety of different surveys, studies, and research have investigated the impact of meditation on aging in general, and DHEA production in particular. Some have claimed astonishing increases in DHEA levels (up to 90 percent) within weeks of subjects learning to meditate. Others have yielded less spectacular, but still impressive changes.

One study that particularly caught my eye, published in the *Journal of Personality and Social Psychology* in 1989, looked at the impact of Transcendental Meditation among the elderly. The research randomly assigned residents of eight homes for the elderly, with an average age of eighty-one, one of four options: Transcendental Meditation, an active thinking program, a relaxation program, and a control group with no program. Short-term findings showed that the meditation group improved the most over a range of physical and mental health measures. However, it was the longer term impact that interested me. After three years, all the members of the meditation group were still alive. Survival rates in the other three groups were all lower. And among those residents who didn't take part in the study the survival rate was only 63 percent.

Exactly why the practice of meditation increases DHEA production is a question that still needs to be answered. But the point is that it does. And at the most basic level, this fact provides a rebuttal to the argument that "I don't have time to meditate," because what are a few minutes spent meditating every morning compared with a few years of robust good health at the end of one's life—and who knows, maybe even years one wouldn't otherwise have had? Quite apart from the many other benefits of meditation, it seems to me that because our only truly finite resource is time, enhancing the quality that we have available to us is just sensible forward planning.

The DHEA finding also prompts interesting questions about what aging really means. The fact that time is subjective is something we often overlook, even though the reality of this is ever-present in our daily life. We all know people who appear or act much older than they are, just as most of us know older people who look significantly younger than their peers. On an experiential level some of us have seen how people's hair can turn white within weeks, even days, after experiencing deep loss. We also hear of "senior" men and women who, embarking on a late-life romance, talk about how they feel like teenagers all over again, experiencing a new lease on life. Perhaps Coco Chanel wasn't far off when she famously declared, "Nature gives you the face you have at twenty; it is up to you to merit the face you have at fifty."

The rate at which we age is not, therefore, predetermined. We are not all following some genetically coded trajectory from which it's impossible to divert. Science has established that through the power of meditation, DHEA output can be increased and the problems of aging delayed. On a subjective level, many of us have an intuitive sense of those activities that make us feel radiantly alive, and those that have the opposite effect. Which is why the physical benefits of meditation are a reflection of the psychological benefits. Like yin and yang, the shape of one determines the other. The physical may appeal to the more empirically inclined among us because it's easier to measure. But the psychological is no less important because it goes to the very heart of how we feel about ourselves and the world around us.

And one of the most exciting developments in recent years has been that, as they have for the physical, scientists have begun to work out ways to monitor, measure, and evaluate the psychological benefits of meditation. An exciting new vista of opportunities is unfolding as cutting-edge technological innovation catches up with ancient mind-training practices, and as Western psychology integrates with Eastern philosophy. The convergence of these dynamics provides us with a more coherent and integrated understanding of human consciousness than has ever previously been possible. We will explore several of these key developments in the next chapter.

CHAPTER THREE

The Psychological Benefits of Meditation

~~~~~~

IT IS A COMMONLY HELD VIEW THAT MEDITATION IS A WAY TO SHUT
OFF THE PRESSURES OF THE WORLD OR OF YOUR OWN MIND, BUT THIS
IS NOT AN ACCURATE IMPRESSION. MEDITATION IS NEITHER SHUTTING
THINGS OUT OR OFF. IT IS SEEING CLEARLY, AND POSITIONING YOUR-
SELF DIFFERENTLY IN RELATION TO THEM.

DR. JON KABAT-ZINN, *WHEREVER YOU GO, THERE YOU ARE:*
MINDFULNESS MEDITATION IN EVERYDAY LIFE

SITTING IN SILENCE with our eyes closed trying to concentrate on just one thing seems, for most of us, an unlikely
route to happiness. In fact, it sounds more like a recipe for
total boredom. Since when has subjecting oneself to sensory
deprivation on a regular basis been an enjoyable or even useful thing to do?

So let's start this chapter with some definitions. In particular, happiness and pleasure, and the difference between the
two. Most of us use the words, and even the concepts behind
the words, interchangeably, so it might be useful to be more
specific.

Pleasure, for the purposes of this book at least, is something that we derive from an object, a place, or person. It is, by
definition, circumstantial. We may get pleasure from dining
in a particular restaurant or driving a new, sleek, up-market
car. But take us to that restaurant after we've just eaten a large

meal, or put us behind the steering wheel during a blazing row with our wife, husband, or significant other, and chances are we will experience no pleasure at all.

If pleasure is a circumstantial enjoyment, happiness refers to a deeper sense of fulfillment not dependent on circumstance, and which is usually accompanied by qualities such as peacefulness, purposefulness, and benevolence. Unlike pleasure, which requires situations to be constantly renewed or upgraded, happiness is a state of mind that grows the more we experience it.

Happy people are those whose essential states are characterized by an abiding fulfillment irrespective of where they happen to be and what they happen to be doing. We recognize truly happy people when we meet them because they are quite rare. They usually have a compelling sense of purpose to their lives, and that purpose is often altruistic. Or as Winston Churchill once observed, "We make a living by what we get, but we make a life by what we give."

Of course happiness is not an all-or-nothing condition, and most of us exist on the spectrum somewhere between the two extremes of meaningless despair and radiant realization. It's also a universal truth that all of us want to move towards the happier end of the spectrum. Yet the simple reality is that we have a strong tendency to pursue pleasure, believing it will provide happiness. Many of us believe the two are the same, or have never given the subject much thought—an amazing notion, given the amount of time and energy we spend trying to achieve self-fulfillment.

Perhaps the reason for our muddle-headedness is that we

tend to stick with what we're good at—filling up our lives with pleasurable distractions. Or perhaps it's just that, by contrast, the strategies for happiness are in relatively short supply.

Our consumerist culture, founded on the pursuit of pleasure, certainly isn't going to give us many clues about true happiness. We may like to think we're too aware, much too sophisticated, to succumb to the relentless tide of advertising that assaults us on a daily basis, trying to persuade us that this particular brand of chocolate, make of car, or holiday experience will make us happier. But, if we're truthful, most of us are victims of the underlying premise that our happiness is dependent on arranging our external world in a particular way—and one that usually involves spending a lot of money!

Even Western psychology has traditionally been less than helpful at promoting happiness given that its focus, like Western medicine, has been on resolving the negatives in our lives, rather than encouraging the development of the positives. To quote Daniel Goleman, author of *Destructive Emotions: How Can We Overcome Them?*: "Psychology has almost entirely dwelt on the problematic, the abnormal, and the ordinary in its focus . . . Very rarely have psychologists . . . shifted their scientific lens to focus on people who were in some sense (other than intellectually) far above normal."

Fortunately, just as the medical community is starting to move to a more holistic understanding of well-being, so too psychologists are taking more of an interest in both the practices and philosophies of Eastern traditions. Instead of settling for "normal neurosis," the state which only a century ago Sigmund Freud believed was a reasonable psychological objective, in recent decades we have begun to discover just how advanced many Eastern traditions are in their understanding of how to fully realize our potential for happiness.

For just as the West, with its focus on the material world, has spent the last two thousand years developing sophisticated technology to manipulate our external reality, by contrast the East, with its focus on the world of the mind, has spent that same time developing highly evolved methods to manipulate our internal reality. In only very recent years has the West developed sufficiently sophisticated equipment to measure the effectiveness of these Eastern traditions, but the results have been truly breathtaking. And perhaps the most exciting findings have concerned the psychological benefits of meditation.

1. REWIRING OUR BRAINS FOR HAPPINESS

Dr. Richard Davidson, director of the Laboratory for Affective Neuroscience at the University of Wisconsin, has played a pioneering role in using the most advanced clinical equipment to monitor the effect of meditation on the brain. Magnetic resonance imaging, or MRI, has long been used in hospitals to provide graphically detailed snapshots of the structure of the brain. A more advanced version of this technology, developed in the early 1990s, is functional MRI (fMRI), which delivers MRI images in video, enabling real-time monitoring of changes in the brain's activity.

Use of fMRI has shown that when people are emotionally distressed—anxious, angry, depressed—the brain's circuits in the right prefrontal cortex are the most active. By way of contrast, when people are happy, energized, or upbeat, activity shifts to the left prefrontal cortex. Having monitored the brain activity of hundreds of subjects, Dr. Davidson found that a baseline reading of activity in the right and left prefrontal areas provided an accurate assessment of a person's mood range. Those people whose activity ranged towards the left tended to be happier, easier-going individuals, while those with more right prefrontal cortex activity tended more towards depression and unhappiness.

Collating the findings of many studies resulted in a typical bell-curve distribution, showing the majority of people in the middle experiencing a mix of good and bad moods. Those occupying the extreme right of the curve were likely to experience clinical depression or anxiety disorder at some time in their life. Those fortunate enough to be on the extreme left were likely to suffer from few bad moods, and would bounce back from them quickly.

The idea that we all have a default "set point" for happiness may at first be surprising. But on reflection, it tends to be confirmed when we look at happiness levels during the course of our own lives. Sure, we all go through bleak periods as well as joyful ones. But the overall level from which we tend towards happiness or sadness is usually constant. If we don't see this in ourselves, it may be easier to see in others, especially those we know well. What's more, we have all encountered people who have an ingrained attitude of hostility, victimization, or defeat, just as we less often come across others who always manage to find a positive interpretation no matter what life throws at them.

The "set point" hypothesis is certainly borne out in studies of mood range which have shown that people's self-reported happiness remained about the same even after major negative or positive life events. Investigating subjects ranging from an individual who was left paraplegic by a car accident at the one extreme, and a lottery winner at the other, researchers found that a year after even these monumental life events, people's happiness levels had changed little.

What is really interesting is that along with the revelation that we may all have a default "set point" for happiness comes the finding that this point can be moved. Dr. Kabat-Zinn, founder of the Mindfulness-Based Stress Reduction Clinic at the University of Massachusetts Medical School, collaborated in a study with Dr. Davidson to assess the impact of mindfulness meditation.

In the study, Dr. Kabat-Zinn taught mindfulness methods to employees of a biotech business for approximately three hours a week over a two-month period. Before the training, the workers complained of feeling highly stressed, a subjective assessment confirmed during fMRI scanning when they showed a collective tendency to the right of the happiness spectrum. By the end of the training period, however, on average their emotions ratio had shifted leftwards, to the positive end of the spectrum. On a personal basis, they reported feeling more energized, less anxious, and more purposeful about their work. Even in a relatively short period of time, inexperienced meditators can begin to alter their overall mood state. So what happens if we keep on meditating?

Dr. Davidson had the good fortune to meet a highly experi-

enced meditator, a senior Tibetan lama, who agreed to undergo
the fMRI process. It should come as no surprise that of the 175
people he had tested until that time, the lama was positioned
on the most extreme left of the happiness spectrum.

Subsequent work carried out at the W. M. Keck Laboratory for Functional Brain Imaging and Behavior involved wir-
ing up volunteers to an electroencephalograph (EEG), a net of
256 electrical sensors, while they meditated. Ten student volunteers with no meditation training were used as a control
group whose readings were to be compared with eight highly
advanced practitioners who were Tibetan monks.

The results of the study were dramatic. While the control
group showed a slight increase in gamma wave activity when
they were asked to meditate, readings from the monks showed
much greater activation of fast-moving and unusually powerful gamma waves. What's more, wave movement through their
brains was far more efficiently organized. Those monks who
had spent the most years meditating had the highest levels
of gamma waves, with some of them producing wave activity
more powerful than had ever been recorded previously.

This "dose response," reported in the *Washington Post*, helps
establish a clear case of cause and effect. In simple terms, the
more we meditate, the better we get at it, and the happier we
feel. Why this might be possible can be explained in terms
of neuroplasticity. While in the past scientists have believed
that the connections between brain nerve cells were fixed
once we reached adulthood, this assumption has been over-
turned. Instead, researchers now understand that the cir-
cuitry and inner workings of the brain continue to develop

and evolve. To quote Dr. Davidson: "What we have found is that the trained mind, or brain, is physically different from the untrained one."

While even fairly small doses of meditation have a positive effect on our moods, continuing the practice opens up new neural pathways, physically reshaping our brains, and shifting our default mood "set point" to the left. In short, meditation rewires us for happiness.

Having meditated for fourteen years I have no doubt at all that I enjoy a much greater degree of equanimity, happiness, and inner peace than I did before. As I'm not aware of a version of myself in a parallel universe who has had identical experiences as me, except for the meditation, I can't prove this point. But I think Dr. Davidson's research has effectively confirmed what I know personally to be true.

For me, it is not so much a sense of ongoing euphoria. I do not leap out of bed every morning singing "Zippity doo-dah!" But unlike my premeditation days when my inner world was shaped by my career, writing ambitions, personal relationships, and financial concerns, the direct, first-hand experience of myself I have acquired through meditation makes me see all those things from a somewhat different perspective. Sure, these same activities are important in a worldly sense. But they don't even begin to define who or what I am. They are necessarily transient, ever-changing and superficial. They are only the waves on the surface, not the infinite ocean that rests beneath.

To give an example of this happiness rewiring at work, a short while ago I invested rather a lot of money in a biotech company which was developing an antiobesity product. While my preference has always been to invest in stock markets through managed funds rather than direct shares, I occasionally invest directly if I have particular knowledge of a company and believe it has an exciting future. And I certainly believed in this one, which was at an advanced stage of clinical trials. If the trial results came back positive, as a procession of scientists, analysts, and medical experts assured us they would, the value of the shares could easily go up as much as 50 percent in the short term, and perhaps as much as two or three times that amount if the wonder drug was snapped up by one of the major pharmaceutical companies.

You will already have guessed how this particular investment ended. I can still remember the sense of total surreality as I opened the company announcement advising the market that the expected rooster had turned out to be a feather duster. Shares instantly lost 70 percent in value.

That evening when my wife offered me a drink, I suggested we crack open a bottle of bubbly. We had lost a lot of money and I thought we ought to mark the occasion. Enjoying champagne seemed an appropriately defiant gesture.

As we sat on the veranda with our drinks, we talked through the whys and wherefores of the transaction. Was there anything I could learn from the experience? Should I have done things differently? Had I been sucked in by the hype?

Although we started the evening feeling decidedly flat, by the end of it we had concluded that despite the day's events we still had cause to celebrate. And it wasn't the temporary effects of the champagne, because our conclusion held true the next day. It was our incredibly good fortune, we decided, that we could afford to lose that amount of money and for it to not affect our lifestyle significantly. Tomorrow, next week, next month, we'd carry on doing exactly as we'd planned to do. Yes, the financial loss did affect investment plans for the future. But we've also had a few wins along the way, and you can't win them all.

You might argue that a person could have reached that same conclusion without the benefit of any meditative experience, and you'd be absolutely right. But we are not talking about "a person," we are talking about me. I know that in a different time and place, without the benefit of meditation—and, it should be said, a very understanding wife—I would probably have reacted very differently, perceiving what had happened to be an unmitigated disaster, a defeat casting a long, dark shadow over the future. I would have allowed the specter of failure to haunt me for months.

As it happens, I feel like one of those Formula One drivers who emerges from the blazing wreckage of his car unscathed. Crashing wasn't a happy experience, but it's already in the past and I've moved on—just, I suspect, like the "set point" in my prefrontal cortex!

2. Moving to a better mental neighborhood

LIFE CAN BE FOUND ONLY IN THE PRESENT MOMENT. THE PAST IS GONE, THE FUTURE IS NOT YET HERE, AND IF WE DO NOT GO BACK TO OURSELVES IN THE PRESENT MOMENT, WE CANNOT BE IN TOUCH WITH LIFE.
THICH NHAT HANH, *THE HEART OF UNDERSTANDING*

Given the choice, none of us would voluntarily live in a rundown, dangerous suburb if we had the option of an up-market neighborhood where the people, parks, and retail amenities were more to our liking. Yet some of us choose to live in very dodgy mental neighborhoods. And like many of the residents of real-life ghettos, we somehow convince ourselves that this is normal, or it's our lot, or there's really nothing we can do about it.

To explain this provocative idea we must refer to mindfulness—one of the key skills we learn from meditation. This life-changing practice has been defined by Dr. Kabat-Zinn in his book *Wherever You Go, There You Are: Mindfulness Meditation in Everyday Life* in the following way: "Mindfulness means paying attention in a particular way: on purpose, in the present moment, and nonjudgmentally. This kind of attention nurtures greater awareness, clarity, and acceptance of present-moment reality. It wakes us up to the fact that our lives unfold only in moments. If we are not fully present for many of those moments, we may not only miss what is most valuable in our lives but also fail to realize the richness and the depth of our possibilities for growth and transformation."

The simple reality is that most of the time we don't monitor the content of our thoughts. We do not live mindfully. From the moment we awaken in the morning until the moment we fall asleep, the mad monkey of the mind is on a constant, agitated romp—much of it of little value, and a lot of it potentially damaging. Most of the time, the mad monkey's activities go completely unchecked and unsupervised. Only sometimes does it focus on the matter at hand.

Of all the working hours we spend sitting in front of our computer screens, for example, how much is truly productive activity, and how much do we waste checking our bank account, the latest web news, the weather in Bali, e-mailing friends, *anything* to avoid getting on with our work? And that's when we're supposed to be concentrating!

Even if we are highly disciplined thinkers at work, what happens when we get home? When we sit down to eat a favorite meal, do we ever savor more than a few mouthfuls before the mad monkey is off again, swinging from the crisis about to engulf one of our clients, to the kids' parties next weekend, to the cat—has it been fed?—to the latest report on climate change? Were a speaker system ever to be attached to our heads, and the ranting incoherence of our thoughts broadcast to all and sundry, how long would we last until the men in white coats arrived to take us away? Would our loved ones, friends, and colleagues ever think of us in quite the same way again? Worse still, would we be unmasked as the most appallingly self-interested individuals, burning off so much of our agitated mental energies on the comfort, anxieties, desires, and obsessions of only one being—me, myself, and I?

For the sake of balance, let's be clear that we all need time for reflection and planning. And no one is disputing that stimulating conversation over the dinner table makes the overall experience more enjoyable.

But what's being described here is a far more pervasive state of being. Something we've grown up with. A tendency so habitual that, like the residents of the dodgy suburb, we think that agitation and indiscipline is normal, or it's our lot, or that there's really nothing we can do about it.

There are two mental neighborhoods we all frequent which

put our equanimity especially at risk. The first of these is The Past, with its particular black spots, including: If Only He/She Hadn't Left Me; They Destroyed My Happiness; I'll Never Get Over It. How much of our thinking time, wherever we are and whatever else we are doing, is spent dwelling on what could or should have been? Playing and replaying conversations, arguments, and previous events. Thinking of the poignant words or killer arguments we might have used. Reawakening those old, familiar, and entirely destructive feelings of desolation or bitterness or "if only . . ." Or, alternatively, thinking back nostalgically to a rose-tinted past including relationships and places we can never recapture, thereby sabotaging our ability to be content in the present moment.

In just a flash, however, we can transport ourselves to that other dangerous suburb, The Future, with its own host of trouble spots such as: When I Am Twenty Pounds Lighter I'm Going to . . . ; If I Could Afford the New Montero . . . ; Tomorrow I'll Show That Bitch/Bastard . . .

The one mental suburb where we tend not to spend so much time is, paradoxically, the one which holds the greatest potential for happiness: The Present. Even though right here and right now is usually a pretty good place to be, instead of abiding in contentment in our experience of the moment, we have a crazily self-destructive impulse to go looking for trouble elsewhere.

A number of respected psychologists agree about the dangers of spending our time in the past, or the future, and give some interesting insights. Daniel Kahneman, who won the Nobel Prize in Economics in 2002 for his insights into irrationality and decision-making, emphasizes the importance of "online" happiness—or how we feel in this moment. The past is not a reliable place to be, he explains, because our memories are flawed. We may spend hours at a wonderful party, but if two drunken guests get into a vicious argument towards the end, we're likely to remember the event as a complete disaster. To create some sense out of life's thousands of disconnected moments, we have an "evaluating self," which focuses on the most intense, or final, moments of an experience, creating a faulty memory which, if relied upon, can lead us to make counterproductive future decisions.

Daniel Gilbert, Professor of Psychology at Harvard University, has shown that we are very bad at predicting how we'll feel in the future. On the one hand, we have a tendency to overestimate the impact of a positive event, believing that a different relationship or new career will result in permanent change, instead of short-term contentment. On the other hand, we underestimate our ability to bounce back from even the most traumatic events, such as the death of someone we love, bankruptcy, or a bitter divorce.

Why do we continue to spend so much of our thoughts in the past or future? Quite possibly because we're not in control. Conditioned to accept mental agitation as normal, most of us don't have the strategies or skills to spend our thinking time on the right side of the tracks. However, the meditation tool of mindfulness is a direct opponent to our usual mental mayhem.

For most of us, when we start to apply mindfulness it's the very first time we've ever paid specific attention to what we're thinking, right now. And the results of this internal, subjective "research" are quite extraordinary. Because we start to understand, at a profound level, the reality that our life is composed of a number of moments, and those moments we don't experience—because we're too busy thinking about something else—can never be recaptured. But by focusing purposefully on what's happening, we fully experience the here and now. The intensity and enjoyment with which we experience individual moments greatly increases.

In much of these first few chapters I have focused on how by "doing" meditation we can expect certain positive results. While this is true, it's also important to understand that meditation is not as much about "doing" as it is about "being." It is the recognition that the present is the only thing that currently exists—all else is mental fabrication.

To quote Dr. Kabat-Zinn in *Wherever You Go, There You Are: Mindfulness Meditation in Everyday Life*: "When we let go of wanting something else to happen in this moment, we are taking a profound step towards being able to encounter what is here now. If we hope to go anywhere or develop ourselves in any way, we can only step from where we are standing. If we don't really know where we are standing—a knowing that comes directly from the cultivation of mindfulness—we may only go in circles, for all our efforts and expectations."

"Living in the moment" or "living in the now" has become a dreadful New Age cliché, sometimes accompanied by flaky imagery involving young children dancing barefoot in dandelion fields, romantic couples at sunset, or other such schmaltzy nonsense which misses the point completely. For no matter how mundane our surroundings, mindfulness can be skill-fully applied to good effect. As we sit at our workstation, are we likely to experience more contentment by seething about a spat at the water cooler, or taking a deep breath, focusing on the sensation of the air passing in and out of our lungs? Standing at the kitchen sink washing dishes, instead of ago-nizing about our body shape and the terrible impression we're going to make at the party next weekend, wouldn't we be bet-ter off focusing on the pleasantly warm feeling of soapy water on our hands?

As Dr. Kabat-Zinn notes, when we practice mindfulness we not only derive far more out of our everyday activities, we also become clearer about what is valuable in our lives. Instead of being caught up in the swirl of flawed memories or equally faulty expectations, we experience much more fully the only thing that is truly real.

And just as the physical benefits of meditation continue long after formal practice has stopped, so too mindfulness practice isn't something that ends when we get off the cushion. In fact, of all the meditation techniques we can learn, this is the most important to carry into everyday life. Not only so we can move to a better mental neighborhood, but also because by living mindfully we create possibilities for even greater per-sonal transformation.

3. Replacing negative thinking with positive

WHETHER YOU BELIEVE THAT YOU CAN, OR BELIEVE THAT
YOU CAN'T, YOU ARE RIGHT.
HENRY FORD, FOUNDER OF THE FORD MOTOR COMPANY

One of the biggest positive changes that meditation has made for me is in the way I interpret what happens to me. And I'm often struck by the paradox that the exciting "new" direction called Cognitive Behavior Therapy I first came across as a second-year psychology student in the 1980s turned out to be one of Buddha's teachings from two and a half thousand years ago. Once again, East and West find common ground.

The way the process works is, on one level, quite simple. We all encounter things in our daily life which make us feel pleased, irritated, grateful, resentful, whatever. We all assume that the way we feel is a normal, even inevitable, consequence of what just happened to us. We're dead wrong.

What we're overlooking is the all-important step that comes *between* our experience of the real-life event, and the way we feel about it. Our interpretation may be instant, visceral, or far more complex, but there can be no emotion without the interpretation that precedes it. To use an everyday example: we have rushed down to the supermarket to pick up some strawberries for the dessert we're planning to serve friends arriving for supper in half an hour. We are, as usual, pressed for time. Hurrying back from the fresh fruit section, we are about to join the checkout line when a woman with a basket laden with groceries rushes to beat us to it, forcing us to wait behind her.

Irritation and indignation may be our entirely predictable

response. We may very well spend the next three minutes steaming with resentment because of the selfish cow. We have no doubt at all that *she's* the cause of our anger. Anyone else in the same situation as us would feel exactly the same way. Wouldn't they? In reality, the reason we're mightily pissed off has much more to do with our thinking than we realize. Consciously or not, our anger is based on thoughts such as:

- It's unbelievably selfish for someone with a full basket of groceries to push in front of someone with just one item!
- She could see I was in a hurry, but she pushed in first—what sort of person does that?
- I'm under pressure—I've a hundred things to do before my friends arrive in half an hour.

These thoughts can quickly escalate and be compounded:

- If I don't get back in ten minutes, I won't have time to do X, Y, and Z, and things will get off to a really bad start.
- I should have picked up the strawberries with all the other stuff earlier. I'm a useless host/hostess.
- Typical! Why does this kind of thing always happen to me?
- Just look at the silly woman and the clothes she's wearing— who does she think she is?
- If I'd joined the other line I would be at the checkout by now.
- The evening is already turning into a disaster thanks to her!

Written down in a list like this, the inherent absurdity of some of these thoughts starts to become apparent. But can we honestly say we don't experience such thoughts sometimes? Maybe even quite frequently?! And this is just the small stuff— the woman pushing into the supermarket line. What about the heavy-duty issues: relationships, work, money? With thinking patterns like these, is it any wonder that we get so stressed out and unhappy?

Interestingly, we all tend to have negative interpretations which have become so habitual that they kick in almost automatically. Albert Ellis, creator of Rational Emotive Behavior Therapy, points out that a lot of us have a tendency to ignore the positive, exaggerate the negative, and overgeneralize, blowing up small problems out of all proportion, turning them into "I always," "You always," "I never," "You never" thinking.

All very well, but you may be wondering what any of this has to do with the benefits of meditation. The connection is that the mindfulness and awareness we learn to develop in meditation (see Chapter 4) are extremely useful tools to use outside of formal sessions. The psychological benefits of meditation don't only apply for the period each day that we meditate. The practice has a ripple effect across our whole way of thinking.

Someone with only poor mindfulness of their own thoughts, which, like mad monkeys, hoot and clamor through their minds unchallenged, can't possibly control them. We have to know the nature of a problem before we can deal with it. By contrast, the person with a more evolved level of mindfulness recognizes the thoughts as they arise and, in so doing, is able to replace negative interpretations of a particular situation with more positive ones.

Thus the mindful strawberry-purchaser, finding himself in exactly the same situation at the checkout line, may think:

- The extra few minutes it'll take to get out of here are of no consequence. Anyway, my supper guests may well arrive late.
- Even if they do arrive on time, they really won't mind if I spend a couple more minutes in the kitchen.
- When I arrived at the store I had no idea how long the lines were going to be. Things could actually be a whole lot worse.
- I don't know what's with the woman in front. Perhaps she's even more pressed for time than I am. But if she acts as self-ishly as this with everyone, she must be a pretty unhappy person. I should actually feel sorry for her.
- After my hectic day, the next few minutes are an opportunity for a quick "spot meditation" (see Chapter 6). I will be mindful of my breathing and relax, so that when I get home I'll feel refreshed and all set for the evening.

There's nothing particularly Pollyanna-ish about these thoughts. They are certainly more useful than the anger-causing alternatives. And the result, for the person experiencing them, is infinitely preferable. If we're completely honest with ourselves, we'll admit that we're just as capable of choosing the positive as the negative interpretations depending on what kind of mood we're in. Glowing with good feeling after we've been paid some kind of compliment, we are far more likely to give people the benefit of the doubt than if we're smoldering over some perceived slight. Whatever our current mood, however, without mindfulness we are choiceless—condemned to remain the helpless victims of our mad-monkey minds, to experience emotionally charged negativity in all its many vivid and exotic forms.

It's also worth noting that we are not the only beneficiaries of more mindful thinking—the people around us are, too. How many times, to continue the case study, have we observed our mother, wife, or other hostess getting more and more agitated preparing for a lunch/dinner/whatever because everything isn't the way she wanted it to be? And do her guests really care? Wouldn't they rather arrive to find their hostess relaxed than stressed out from trying to make everything accord with her own particular idea of perfection—which may be very different from theirs anyway?

The shopping illustration is deliberately mundane, because we've all been there. But exactly the same process applies to the much bigger challenges in our lives: the loss of a lover, partner, or close friend. Business failure or financial betrayal. The discovery that I am, or someone close to me is, suffering from a life-threatening disease. Can mindfulness really help us in situations as dire as these? Surely positive interpretations aren't even possible in these circumstances? In fact, it's in our darkest moments that practicing mindfulness is more relevant than ever, because these are exactly the times we are most likely to think and talk ourselves into unnecessary suffering.

A few years ago a friend of mine—let's call her Lizzy—went through the truly awful experience of being told by her husband—let's call him Jim—that he was leaving her for another woman. After twenty-one years together, during which they'd shared every aspect of their lives, her feelings of betrayal and rejection were hard enough to cope with. But the practical and financial consequences were frightening too. Suddenly she was losing her family home and a large proportion of her retirement savings. Not only would she have to radically revise her work plans, but for most of the time she'd also need to be the single parent to their teenage son.

To begin with, she felt overwhelming anger at the betrayal, and intensely jealous of her ex-husband's apparently blissful new relationship. The very sight of him made her feel physically nauseous—she told him to keep away.

But as a longtime practitioner of mindfulness and meditation she knew that allowing herself to become consumed with bitterness wasn't hurting her ex one bit—but it was seriously damaging her own peace of mind. "I got to the point where I realized it was pointless focusing on what he'd done. I couldn't change that and thinking about it only made me angry. What really mattered was focusing on what *I* could do, how *I* chose to think. I knew if I wanted to have happy, successful relationships in the future, I couldn't allow myself to feel bitter about the past. And I couldn't allow my negativity to start harming my son."

Which is why Lizzy began to change her interpretations of what had happened, self-consciously and step-by-step. Every time she had a negative thought, she'd counter it with a positive one. If she found herself getting angry with her ex, she'd deliberately cultivate the thought, "I should be happy for Jim. He's basically a nice person and he's getting so much happiness from this relationship." Feeling resentment about her circumstances she'd remind herself, "I may be in a more difficult situation than before, but there are a lot of people far worse off than me."

Feeding negative emotions had made them powerful and all-consuming, says Lizzy. But the opposite was also true. By deliberately switching to positive thoughts, however contrived and artificial it felt to begin with, the negativity quickly shrank back: "When you focus on positive thoughts, negative emotions can't exist. They just disappear. You find yourself feeling negativity less and less."

Interestingly, one of the biggest obstacles to this practice came from Lizzy's friends and colleagues. "They hated Jim for what he'd done and didn't want me to have any positive thoughts about him. But I wasn't thinking positively for his sake. I was doing it for my own happiness, and for my son's."

When Lizzy told me all this, I congratulated her on her saintly behavior. But she was quick to shrug off my praise. Once again she emphasized how replacing negative attitudes with positive ones, while one of the hardest challenges of her life, had been motivated by her wish for personal happiness, and the wish to be a good mother. She didn't set out to be benevolent towards her ex-husband. But she knew that thinking benevolently was in her own best interests. "One of the biggest motivators to change my mind was the pain of my own suffering. You either remain a slave to your suffering, or you change it.

If most people would recognize that they have the ability to change their minds, then their journey would begin."

None of this would have been possible without a certain level of mindfulness. Had Lizzy been trapped in a tumult of rage, she would have had no capacity to identify self-destructive thinking, much less effect change. She would have been condemned to live in a particularly dark and horrific mental neighborhood, constantly assaulted by jealousy, recrimination, anxiety, and anger.

But with mindfulness comes the ability to take control of our mental destiny; the opportunity to reshape our emotional landscape completely. The transformative power of mindfulness is one of the greatest benefits we can acquire through meditation, whether on or off our cushions. It is also undoubtedly one of life's greatest prizes because in making us stronger and more resilient it sets us free.

THE SOCIAL BENEFITS OF MEDITATION

THE QUAKER CONVICTION IS THAT AS WE GO DEEPER INTO OURSELVES WE SHALL EVENTUALLY REACH A STILL, QUIET CENTER. AT THIS POINT TWO THINGS HAPPEN SIMULTANEOUSLY. EACH OF US IS AWARE OF OUR UNIQUE VALUE AS AN INDIVIDUAL HUMAN BEING, AND EACH OF US IS AWARE OF OUR UTTER INTERDEPENDENCE ON ONE ANOTHER.
GEORGE GORMAN, QUAKER WRITER

Because meditation has only started becoming mainstream in the West during recent years, comparatively little work has been done to identify what happens to a society when an increasing number of individuals begin practicing meditation.

But initial studies have been undertaken, revealing intriguing results and suggesting that this area may offer rich opportunities for further investigation. Although this chapter's focus is on personal rather than social benefits, for the sake of completeness I'd like to briefly refer to the latter here.

Within the overall population there are some groups that are more problematic than others. One such group comprises convicted criminals, and this is an area where considerable research has been done studying the impact of teaching offenders Transcendental Meditation (TM) techniques, either in jail or instead of going to jail. The TM premise is essentially a simple one: recidivism rates are reduced when individual offenders develop greater levels of self-awareness and self-control, better moral judgment, less anxiety and aggression, and less likelihood of substance abuse. The benefits to society are a lower crime rate, and potential cost savings in the police, courts, and prison systems.

During the past three decades, thirty-nine studies have been conducted on the rehabilitative effects of the TM program, and overall they provide compelling evidence that the TM premise works. For example, Dr. Charles Alexander's groundbreaking doctoral work at the Massachusetts Correctional Institute in Walpole studied recidivism rates among former inmates who had learned TM in jail. Following the former inmates over fifteen years he compared recidivism rates to those of a control sample and found that the risk of recidivism dropped by 43 percent among those who'd learned TM. Other studies have shown recidivism reductions between 30 and 40 percent.

"Enlightened Sentencing" or therapeutic jurisprudence is

where offenders receive counseling and TM training instead of being put behind bars. Clearly this can only be applied in specific cases where individuals don't automatically deserve a jail term—for example, where their anger has got them into trouble with the law. In Australia, Dr. Michael King, a magistrate in Geraldton, has been a pioneer of introducing TM through Enlightened Sentencing which he says has been shown to reduce recidivism by over 40 percent. Speaking on ABC Radio he said, "In our program, we've found that it makes people more relaxed, more balanced in themselves, better able to engage with the program overall. So it contributed to the effectiveness of each of the other rehabilitation programs."

While statistics are important—and it's hard to knock a statistic like a 40 percent improvement—the social impact of significantly reduced recidivism goes way beyond spreadsheet figures. Commenting on the impact of teaching TM in jails, Judge David C. Mason of St. Louis, Missouri, says, "I have the benefit of seeing its effect on offenders I have placed on probation. They are demonstrating greater self-esteem and self-control. Their mothers, girlfriends, and wives speak in glowing terms of the 'new' man in their lives . . . One offender actually advised another to plead guilty only if assigned to my court so that he might get into the Transcendental Stress Management program (The Enlightened Sentencing Project)." There are very many other such endorsements by judges and prison officers as well as offenders themselves.

It was in response to this same human need that Tibetan Buddhist nun Venerable Robina Courtin launched The Liberation Prison Project, in which over three thousand five hundred offenders in over five hundred prisons both in the US and worldwide are provided with meditation teachings, study groups, and other support. While the meditations and teachings are Tibetan Buddhist rather than TM, there is a common rehabilitative process, and clear evidence that in helping individuals turn their prisons into monasteries, the human and social dividend can be significant.

Still on the subject of crime, the TM organization has also gathered evidence that meditation impacts on broader social well-being too. Named "the Maharishi effect" in honor of Maharishi Mahesh Yogi, founder of TM, when over 1 percent of a given population practices TM, it is suggested that a variety of positive social changes occur. One of the most easily measured of these is a reduction in the crime rate. Experiments have been conducted in which large numbers of TM practitioners have moved to a particular location for a specific period to boost local meditator numbers, and crime rates have been carefully monitored. During a demonstration of "the Maharishi effect" in July 1993, over four thousand TM practitioners gathered in Washington, DC. A twenty-seven-member independent team of scientists and community leaders found a 21 percent reduction in violent crimes for the period in question (Dubrovnik Peace Project).

The 1 percent hypothesis is certainly an interesting one, but given that any large town or city in the developed world would struggle to find 1 percent of any kind of regular meditator—TM or otherwise—it will probably be some time before the broader social impacts of meditation can be more fully explored. Nevertheless, as meditation becomes increasingly widely practiced, both among defined groups as well as the broader population, further social benefits are likely to emerge: we should expect the unexpected.

CHAPTER FOUR

How to Meditate: The Nuts and Bolts

SIT, THEN, AS IF YOU WERE A MOUNTAIN, WITH ALL THE UNSHAK-
ABLE, STEADFAST MAJESTY OF A MOUNTAIN. A MOUNTAIN IS COM-
PLETELY NATURAL AND AT EASE WITH ITSELF, HOWEVER STRONG THE
WINDS THAT TRY TO BATTER IT, HOWEVER THICK THE DARK CLOUDS
THAT SWIRL AROUND ITS PEAK. SITTING LIKE A MOUNTAIN, LET YOUR
MIND RISE AND FLY AND SOAR.

SOGYAL RINPOCHE, *THE TIBETAN BOOK OF LIVING AND DYING*

"CAN YOU show me how to meditate?" I am sometimes asked by a friend or acquaintance. It's clear from their expression that they're a bit apprehensive about what they're getting into. Perhaps it's the religious overtones that medita-tion has for some people. Or is it an association with those classified advertisements you sometimes see offering the ambiguous prospect of tantric relaxation?

Fear not, dear reader. If you've gotten this far, you'll have realized that this book is not about religious or any other kind of ecstasy. Meditation can be a powerful and life-changing practice—but the core instructions, the nuts and bolts of it, are actually very simple. And they can be followed fully clothed.

WHERE AND WHEN?

A quiet room with the door shut, first thing in the morning, is the recommended where and when of meditation. Until we get to be very advanced meditators, able to withdraw from external stimuli, it helps to be able to shut them out physically if at all possible. And first thing in the morning suits most people because after a good night's sleep we tend to be more refreshed, and our minds less cluttered, than in the evening. The Sanskrit term for the early morning is *amrit vela*, or "time of nectar." Since ancient times Indian yogis have believed this to be the optimal time to practice meditation, and more recently it has been suggested by Western science that this is the time when important hormones of the pituitary gland are secreted. By assisting this process through meditation, we set up our hormonal balance for the day ahead.

Because I take a while to fully wake up in the mornings, my own particular routine is to get up and take a shower before meditating. But there are few dos and don'ts applying to the where and when of meditation, apart from common sense and what suits your personal temperament.

I have read accounts, for example, of prisoners who have taken up meditation despite living in shared cells, and having to put up with constant noise, agitation, and personally directed abuse. Their fortitude in sticking with the practice, despite such conditions, is to be admired.

If there is no possibility of your being able to meditate until getting kids off to school, or even until the end of the day, don't use this as a reason not to start meditating. And if the laundry room or garden shed is the only place to avoid noise and interruptions, then welcome to your new meditation sanctuary!

For how long?

For how long should you meditate? I would suggest you start with ten or fifteen minutes. It's important that meditation is not a chore for you, but something you want to do, at the very least a matter of curiosity, hopefully developing into the source of greatly enhanced inner peace. Ideally we should end a session feeling positively about what we've just done, instead of relieved it's all over. By starting with bite-size chunks, we will want to increase the length of our sessions quite naturally as our concentration improves. While some meditators put a watch in front of them to keep track of time, if you find this creates a distraction, you may like to use an alarm clock. I have a friend who does this—leaving the clock in the next room so she doesn't get too startled when it goes off!

Posture

The seven-point meditation posture has been used for at least two and a half millennia and across most meditative traditions. It goes—almost—without saying that before assuming the following posture, for the sake of comfort you should remove your shoes and loosen any tight clothing, such as belts and ties. Ideal meditation clothing is simply a T-shirt or sweatshirt, shorts or tracksuit pants, or a comfortable dressing gown.

If you can't adopt the posture outlined, for example because of an injury, troublesome joints, or some other physical disability, this doesn't mean you can't meditate. As outlined below, a normal seating posture will also provide a perfectly useful basis to begin. Even if you are confined to bed, so long as you are able to maintain a straight spine, you have the most essential element to begin meditation. In fact, you may find the body scanning meditation technique described in Chapter 5 particularly useful and/or enjoyable.

1 Sit cross-legged on a cushion on the floor. The purpose of the cushion, which should be firm, is to tilt the pelvis so it's easier and more comfortable to sit over a longer period of time. Having three points of contact—the butt and both knees— provides good stability. While meditation cushions are gen-

erally available on-line, in specialty shops, or from meditation centers, to get started you may want to try out a few different cushion alternatives from your home until you find one that provides comfortable but firm support.

Some meditators prefer to use a low wooden stool on which they sit, essentially in a kneeling position, with their legs tucked behind them. Alternatively, they kneel astride a cushion. If sitting cross-legged is very difficult or painful for you, these postures provide another option.

If neither the cross-legged nor meditation stool posture is possible for you, you can simply sit on a chair or bench. In this case it's recommended that you cross your legs between knees and ankles.

From time to time, whether sitting cross-legged or in a chair, you may want to alternate which foot/leg is in front. This helps even out any imbalance in your posture.

Some meditators use a mat, rug, or carpet under their cushion, so that their knees don't press into the hard floor. However, this pressure is only likely to become painful if you have long meditation sessions, which will not apply to begin with.

2 Rest your hands in your lap. The three most common hand positions are:

- resting palm down, one on each knee.
- resting one on each knee, palm up. The tips of thumb and index or middle finger may be held together.
- resting with the right hand in the left, palms upwards, like a pair of shells, and thumb tips meeting approximately at the level of the navel.

Most teachers and groups have their own preferences, but I am not aware that any of the above alternatives has advantages over others. Try them out for yourself and see which feels more comfortable.

3 Keep your back straight. Of all the posture instructions, this is the most important because your spine is the main conduit of your central nervous system. Your back should be straight, but following its natural tendency to be slightly curved in the lower back. When you meditate, it's important to keep the spine relaxed, neither slumped nor artificially straight. This straight-back instruction holds true whether one is sitting on a meditation cushion or a regular chair, or even lying in bed.

4 Relax your shoulders. Ideally they should be slightly rolled back, down, and resting level. Arms therefore rest loosely by your sides, not held tightly in.

5 Tilt the head slightly forward. Keeping the head evenly balanced, tuck your chin slightly inwards. Tilt angle can be a useful control. If your mind is going particularly crazy, try deepening the tilt, moving your face down towards the floor. If, on the other hand, you start to feel very sleepy, try lifting your head, like a sunflower, to get rid of drowsiness.

6 Relax your face. Your mouth, jaw, and tongue should be neither slack nor tight and your brow should be smooth. By placing the tip of the tongue behind your front teeth, you can help control the buildup of saliva.

7 **Close your eyes.** Not too tightly, just gently resting your eyelids. While keeping your eyes half-opened, unfocused, and gazing downwards is recommended for some kinds of meditation, at the beginning most people find that keeping the eyes fully closed is better for eliminating distraction.

Begin with an objective in mind

Now that you're in position, you've checked your posture, and you're all set, what happens next? To give structure to your practice it's a good discipline to work out a stated objective, in the form of an affirmation, which you use both to begin and end the session. The statement of this objective is very important and worth spending some time considering before you start your meditation sessions. It should encapsulate what you're wishing to achieve from meditation in a way that's powerful to you. Some suggestions on how to phrase your objective/affirmation are as follows.

Make it personal. Not everyone is looking for the same thing from meditation. Some people are looking for inner peace and calm. Others want to help heal a serious illness. Still others want to improve their concentration for study and exams. Consider the specific outcome(s) you are looking to achieve.

Make it positive. Express your objective in a positive way. For example, "I won't find it hard to learn my history notes," would be better stated as "I learn my history notes with complete mastery and ease." No to "My bowel cancer will be healed." Yes to "My whole body is in robust good health."

Make it present. The present tense provides the best basis for your objective statement. "By the practice of this meditation my whole system is becoming more relaxed and at ease," is better than "This meditation will make me become more relaxed and at ease."

Incorporate others. Research, as well as collective experience, suggests that it's a good idea to incorporate the well-being of others, as well as yourself, into your motivation. As part of the research into the effects of meditation studied via fMRI (see Chapter 3), Dr. Richard Davidson asked experienced meditators to try out a variety of different techniques. There was a significant difference in activity in the left prefrontal cortex of the brain—the part associated with happiness—when the meditators focused on a well-known Buddhist concept called *bodhichitta*, or loving-kindness. On learning the news, the Dalai Lama was delighted to have confirmed what he'd always suspected—that the first beneficiary, when we focus positive thoughts on others, is, paradoxically, ourselves.

If you are meditating to help deal with stress, you might therefore use an affirmation such as:

> By the practice of this meditation
> I am becoming calm and relaxed,
> More efficient and happier in all that I do,
> Both for my own sake as well as for others.

Learn it by heart. Learn the words of your affirmation by heart. There are three good reasons for doing this. First, if you can say them without having to read them, you can focus fully on their meaning, rather than on the process of reading them. Second, the repetition of a suggestion, while in a relaxed state, has a particular power to effect change, and has some similarities in this respect to hypnotherapy. And third, if you have the affirmation down pat, you can mentally repeat it at any time during the day. Having effectively "anchored" a state of relaxed confidence to the phrase during your meditation, merely repeating the phrase can help to recreate the same state, wherever you are and whatever you happen to be doing.

Religious option. If you follow a particular religious tradition, your affirmation could take the form of a prayer. If there is a prayer that particularly moves you, by all means use it to begin your session. If the prayer does not include a clear objective for the session, it would be a good idea to add a line or two at the end, to provide specific focus to what you are about to do.

End as you begin. You can use the same affirmation to wrap up at the end of your meditation session. Doing so reinforces your purpose and also provides a structured close to the session.

Breath counting:
A foundation meditation practice

Turning to the main content of our meditation session, probably the best practice to begin with is breath-counting meditation. This is a practice used widely across meditative traditions, and through all levels from novice meditators to the most advanced students. There are a number of reasons for this. The breath is a convenient object of meditation because we have no difficulty finding it. Making it the focus of our attention is an entirely natural process. When we do, our breathing tends to slow down quite naturally, thereby slowing our entire metabolism and making us feel more relaxed. And achieving a calm but focused state serves as a very useful stabilization practice both in itself and also if we then wish to focus on a more subtle object of meditation (explained further in Chapter 5).

There are some meditative practices originating in India which emphasize the importance of something called *prana*, a Sanskrit word meaning "absolute energy" and thought of as a universal life force. According to the Ayurvedic tradition, an ancient Hindu science of health which sees physical, emotional, and spiritual well-being as interconnected, when we breathe in, we are not just taking more oxygen on board, we are also absorbing *prana*, the vital force sustaining our lives. It can be useful to remind ourselves of this simple but critical fact. My teacher often points out that the only thing separating us from death is the very tenuous process of breathing, a cycle which, for the vast majority of our lives, is something we remain completely unaware of.

With this first breath-counting exercise, our objective is to actively shift our focus to the breath. We do this, quite simply, by mentally counting each breath on exhalation, for a set number of breaths—typically between four and twenty-one—before repeating the exercise.

The process is as follows: place the focus of your attention at the tip of your nostrils, like a sentry, and observe the flow of air as you breathe in, and then out. Ideally all the air you inhale and exhale should be through your nose, with your mouth kept firmly shut. However, if you have a condition that makes this difficult, by all means part your lips slightly to inhale and exhale.

As you breathe out, count the number "one" in your mind, then on the next out-breath "two," then "three," "four," and so on. Don't focus on anything else—for example, don't follow the air travelling into your lungs, or your rib cage rising and falling. Don't allow your mind to wander from the tip of your nostrils. And try not to fall asleep!

As mentioned at the start of this chapter, what we're setting out to achieve is really very simple—but not necessarily easy. The best way to discover this for yourself is to try it. Pretty soon, you'll find all kinds of thoughts demanding your attention. Even though you've set this time aside for meditating, habitual agitation or drowsiness may very soon kick in, to the point that you may discover you can't even count to ten!

This is called gross agitation and it happens to us all. When it does, once you realize you've lost the object of meditation, the breath, simply refocus on it and start back at one again. Try not to beat yourself up about your lapse of attention or fall into the trap of believing that you're one of the few people who can't meditate. Your experience is, in fact, totally normal. Our minds are amazingly inventive at coming up with reasons to avoid self-discipline: you shouldn't buy into any of them!

If you experience a lot of gross agitation in the beginning, don't even attempt a count of ten, but see if you can reach four, then when you feel comfortable with that, perhaps build up to a regular count of seven. When I first started meditating, for many months my main practice was simply to spend ten minutes each day counting to four. It was a simple practice, but one which provided a very strong foundation and was to have far-reaching effects.

Another tip: when doing this particular meditation you may like to include the word "and" on the in-breaths between numbers. This provides our minds with some extra support between the numbers. Though, like the training wheels on a child's first bicycle, you should aim to get rid of the "ands" as your concentration improves.

As this happens, your focus on the breath will become sharper. Try paying more concentrated attention to the detail of your practice. The subtle, physical sensation at the tip of your nostrils as you breathe. The coolness of the air coming in. The warmer sensation as you exhale. You can note the start of each in-breath, how it builds up, then how it tapers off. The gap between in-and out-breaths. Then the start, middle, and fading away of each exhalation. The much longer gap at the end of each exhalation.

As you get into a meditation session, your breathing will probably slow, and you'll become more and more conscious of the gaps between out-breath and in-breath. What do you focus on then? Only the absence of breath and the complete relaxation you experience with nothing to distract you, and no demands being put on you. This may not seem an ambitious goal but, rest assured, it is not only profoundly calming, it is also a stepping stone to other more advanced meditation practices.

AGITATION AND DULLNESS

Early on in your meditation practice you will discover the two main obstacles to meditation— agitation and dullness. Each of these exists on a spectrum from major to minor, or from gross to subtle.

Gross agitation is, for example, the recollection, midway between breath two and breath three, that you have failed to transfer sufficient money to cover a check you wrote two days ago. This leads to your imagining the call you're going to have to make to your bank, the endless automatic prompts you're going to have to follow before you finally end up speaking to a human being, the lack of help or support you're likely to receive, the bounced check fee you'll be forced to pay, and the embarrassment of having to call the recipient and reissue a check.

Heart pounding and palms starting to perspire, you suddenly remember—I'm supposed to be meditating! Where was I? Two? Or three? Unable to remember, you have to bring the mind back, gently but firmly, to start at one again. With gross agitation, you've quite simply lost the plot, or to put it more formally, you lose the object of concentration.

With more subtle agitation you are still able to keep counting your breath, but experience the distraction as background chatter. The more advanced meditator who has failed to transfer money may also have the thought pop into their mind, but instead of giving it any attention, they will continue to focus on their counting, not allowing their concentration to be disturbed. The thought simply dissolves away.

I once heard the story of a writer who decided that a meditation retreat would be just the thing to stimulate some creative thinking. Arriving at his first session with a pen and brand new notepad on which he intended jotting his freshly inspired ideas, he was dismayed when the meditation teacher swooped down, confiscating the tools of his trade. "Our job is to starve our thoughts of attention," the teacher admonished him, "not to develop them!"

This is no easy thing, of course, because it goes against our habitual tendency to focus on a thought before taking that thought in any number of directions. Trying *not* to develop thoughts goes against what we've done all our lives and is actually very hard work.

Every year I try to go on a two-week meditation retreat. When I announce my plans in advance to friends and clients, they will often look at me with envious expressions as though I'd just told them I was heading off to a luxury spa to be pampered in mud baths and fed grapes by scantily clad women. "You're so lucky!" they'll say. "Two weeks of meditation—it must be so *relaxing*."

Yeah, sure, I think to myself. Eight hours a day sitting cross-legged on a meditation cushion trying to counter mental habits so ingrained I can't remember ever not doing them—can it get more relaxing than this?! Seriously, there is a real sense of achievement completing a retreat, but cultivating a relaxed state of being doesn't come naturally to most of us.

On which subject, we turn to that other meditation obstacle, dullness. This is when our concentration is threatened by sleepiness or heaviness. Gross dullness means discovering that we have nodded off completely. On retreat, the first, postlunch session of the afternoon is often a time when minds grow dull, postures slide, and it's even been known for snoring to be heard, before familiar neck-snaps back to concentration. Gross dullness, like gross agitation, means the complete interruption of our meditative concentration.

Subtle dullness ranges from a state of deep—and quite possibly enjoyable—relaxation in which we are nevertheless no longer alert and focused, to an even greater state of relaxation which threatens to turn into sleep. Maintaining the clarity of our focus is the main challenge.

When most people start out meditating, they often find they have a tendency to experience one obstacle rather than the other. We should use common sense to try to reduce any external factors—for example, if we are always overwhelmed with tiredness and we're trying to meditate at 9:00 p.m. every night, could we move our session to an earlier slot? Would a shower beforehand help wake us up?

But apart from trying to get our external environment right, there are two meditation tools which are essential to our practice.

MINDFULNESS AND AWARENESS

DO NOT MISTAKE THE RUNNING COMMENTARY IN YOUR MIND ("NOW
I'M BREATHING IN, NOW I'M BREATHING OUT") FOR MINDFULNESS;
WHAT IS IMPORTANT IS PURE PRESENCE.
SOGYAL RINPOCHE, *THE TIBETAN BOOK OF LIVING AND DYING*

Mindfulness means keeping the object of meditation in your mind and not allowing your concentration to stray. In this case, the object is the sensation of the breath entering and leaving your nostrils. Making sure your focus stays on the breath, and doesn't move, is the application of mindfulness.

Awareness means being watchful of what your mind is actually doing and safeguarding it from wandering. This may seem very similar to mindfulness, but it's subtly and importantly different.

The best illustration I've heard to explain the difference between mindfulness and awareness is what happens when you carry a very full mug of coffee across a room. The surface of the liquid near the rim of the mug could easily spill over, so you are treading with great care. Mindfulness equates to how you keep a very close watch on the surface of the coffee to make sure it doesn't spill. But as you carry the mug, part of your attention is also taking in the bigger picture, making sure you're not about to trip over the dog or bump your elbow against a doorframe. That part of your attention is awareness. While working towards the same objective as mindfulness, it is nevertheless a slightly different aspect of your consciousness.

When I first began to meditate, I really didn't get the difference between mindfulness and awareness. No one had explained the cup of coffee analogy to me—that came much later, at which time it all started making a lot more sense. But at the beginning, I thought that making a distinction between mindfulness and awareness was really a case of splitting hairs—probably because we tend to use the two words interchangeably in everyday life.

It may also be worth mentioning that I had a hard time with subtle agitation too. Did it really exist? Surely you were either focused on something, or you weren't? My problem in understanding this concept was quite simply that my own mind was so agitated I never knowingly experienced subtle agitation. It was all very much at the major, or gross, level. There I'd be, sitting down to concentrate on my breath counting and, the next thing I knew, I was thinking about a money transfer. I'd have to start again at one. Hardly surprising I thought that subtle agitation was up there with Santa and the tooth fairy.

How mindful should we be when we meditate? Probably the best way to answer this is to quote the Buddha himself when he taught meditation to a famous *vina* player (something like a guitarist) who had become a monk. "How did you get the best sound out of your *vina*? Was it when the strings were very tight or when they were very loose?" Buddha asked him. "Neither. When they had just the right tension, neither too taut nor too slack." 'Well, it's exactly the same with your mind," said Buddha.

We need to practice alert relaxation, or relaxed alertness, when we meditate, watching our minds the whole time. What we want to avoid is concentration that's too "loose," and soon unravels into full-blown distraction, or concentration that's so "tight" that we tense up and give ourselves a headache. And as pointed out by Sogyal Rinpoche, while we are doing this we need to take care we don't allow our own observation of the meditation to become a distraction in itself. How frequently we experience the sensation of achieving a few moments of pure clarity and awareness before realizing we have just pointed this out to ourselves, thereby bringing the experience to an abrupt halt. What we are aiming for is pure presence.

Pure presence is something we can and do achieve. Little by little, and without us even noticing it, the length of our concentration begins to increase so that we can not only count from one to four, but can do so several times before hitting a speed bump. We also begin to notice that our concentration is not a simple binary thing, either on or off but, like the sea, has different qualities or colors to it.

The practice of focusing on just our breath, or on any other chosen object of meditation, is known as "single-pointed concentration" and is the goal of most meditation practices. Sometimes our efforts at single-pointed concentration are hard-won, and we have to focus extremely intently to be mindful of the object of meditation. At other times, it feels less difficult, and while there is a low-level background narrative of thoughts, we are able to ignore these with less effort.

Occasionally, most wonderful of all, are the rare moments when we establish our focus and then simply rest in a state of relaxed concentration, our minds free of distraction, and experience a feeling of clarity, spaciousness, and profound peace. It is moments like these that make all the hard slog worthwhile: transcendent experiences when we are able to rise beyond the usual chatter of self-obsession. It is during these moments, when we find ourselves looking simply and directly at the sky-like quality of our mind, and not the obscuring cloud coverage, that we realize we are beginning to experience what could be our own true nature.

BREATHING MEDITATION CHECKLIST

1 Physical posture Legs are crossed, hands resting, back straight, shoulders rolled back, arms loose by your sides, head tilted slightly down, face relaxed, eyes shut.

2 Psychological posture Give yourself permission not to think about your usual concerns. Be a person, in this moment, with no history and no future.

3 Mentally recite your objective/affirmation You may like to do this three times, focusing on its meaning.

4 Focus attention at the tip of your nostrils Observe the sensation of air moving in and out.

5 Count the breaths on each exhalation From one to four, seven, or ten—choose a cycle and stick to it for the session.

6 Use mindfulness and awareness Remember that the focus of your mind is on your breathing and watch what your mind is really doing.

7 Bring your attention back Do this every time it wanders.

8 Deepen your concentration Focus on how each inhalation begins, builds, and ends; the pause before exhalation; how each exhalation begins, builds, and tapers; the gap at the end of the cycle.

9 Pure presence Be aware of breathing as you breathe. Try to avoid giving yourself a running commentary on the progress of your meditation.

10 End the session However good or bad your concentration during the session, try especially hard to finish like a winner. Then repeat your affirmation. Allow yourself a few moments as you open your eyes, and come back to the room.

CHAPTER FIVE

Different Types of Meditation

~~~~~~

THE POINT IS NOT TO CHANGE OURSELVES. THE POINT IS TO MAKE
FRIENDS WITH WHO WE ALREADY ARE.
PEMA CHÖDRÖN, *THE WISDOM OF NO ESCAPE*

"MEDITATION" is a bit like the word "sport"—football players, pole-vaulters, and golfers are all sportspeople, but what a variety of activities! Underlying the many different types of sports, however, we can identify a number of common elements: cardiovascular fitness, visual–motor coordination, muscular strength, self-discipline, and emotional resilience.

The same, too, with meditation. On the surface of it, the person who sits focusing on counting breaths may seem to be engaged in an altogether different pursuit from the one walking around the garden, who in turn appears to have little in common with the one visualizing being dissolved into healing blue light, but they are all engaged in meditation. They all require strong concentration. Mindfulness and awareness. And, like sportspeople, self-discipline and emotional resilience.

So what are the major types of meditation? As it happens, there is no universally accepted method of classification. How the main practice types are defined depends on the tradition of the practitioner. In the fourteen years I've been meditating, I've come across a number of elaborate and apparently quite rigorous models to categorize the different meditation practices, but there is little clear consensus between them.

In the end, as individual practitioners we find ourselves thinking in terms of two simple categories: those practices we find useful, and those we don't. Yes, it may well be intriguing to know about Zen archery, the mystical pathway of Richard of St. Victor, or the dervish dancers of the Sufi tradition, but most busy Westerners are likely to attain greater benefit from a solid, if unspectacular, course of breath counting.

In providing the following meditation practices, I am not claiming that they provide a definitive list, nor that they constitute some method of classification. Rather, I hope you'll find them a useful "starter kit" to try out for yourself, and to see which practices you find personally helpful. You will almost certainly be drawn to some rather than others, but it's worth experimenting with each one. You may well discover a large degree of complementarity between the different practices. Breathing meditation, for example, can be an excellent way to stabilize the mind before beginning a mindfulness of mind meditation. Analytical, or contemplative, meditation can enhance most other forms of meditation. I have referred to some of these links in my descriptions of the different practices.

Before trying them out, I'd urge you to read Chapter 4, if you haven't already done so, as it provides some of the necessary meditation basics which we'll take as read in this chapter. In each case, I'll assume you are already seated and motivated as previously described.

A definite no-no I should mention at the outset is switching meditation types during the session. Starting off with a visualization exercise before deciding, after five minutes, that you're in the mood for a spot of walking meditation, and then wondering if you can combine this with some analytical practice is no way to develop meditative concentration. Once you have decided on a course of action, stay with it for the whole session. The only exception to this is if you use one practice as a form of "warm-up" to the main event, which I have suggested in several cases.

1. NINE-CYCLE BREATHING MEDITATION

In the previous chapter I described a simple breath-counting meditation. I am including an alternative breathing meditation in this chapter because the benefits of breath-based meditations really can't be overstated, especially when we begin learning to meditate. Briefly restated, these benefits are that the breath is an easy "object" to find; when we focus on it both our breathing and whole metabolism naturally slow, and we are able to achieve a useful state of calm but focused stabilization.

Having tried the breath-based meditation in Chapter 4, you may wish to experiment with this one, which is subtly different. If you like both, feel free to use them during alternate sessions.

To begin this breathing meditation, focus on inhaling through your left nostril and exhaling through your right nostril for three breaths. Then inhale through your right nostril and exhale through your left for three breaths. Finally, inhale and exhale through both nostrils for three breaths, completing the cycle of nine, before starting over.

If you like, you can give physical support to this by placing a thumb and finger on either side of your nose, alternately blocking each nostril as you inhale or exhale. However, this is only an option, not a necessity. The point of this exercise is not so much to breathe through only one nostril, but to practice focusing your attention on each nostril individually.

Because it's a slightly busier meditation than breath counting, you may find it easier to sustain mindfulness. However if you have difficulty breathing through just one nostril, for example because of a cold or sinusitis, this exercise may be better avoided.

As in the case of breath counting, having firmly placed your concentration on the breath, aim to both maintain that concentration and develop it, observing the nature of each in-breath and out-breath, and the spaces in between, as described before.

How it feels: Like breath counting, nine-cycle breath meditation allows us to relax progressively. Enjoy the simplicity of it. Pay close attention not only to every single breath, but to the beginning, middle, and end of each in-breath and out-breath, and to the spaces in between. Having deprived yourself of each nostril alternately, experience the wonderful release of breathing freely through both. The calmness after your exhalation tapers and you are mindful simply of the absence of breath. By abiding in this nonduality of breath and mind you can enjoy a wonderfully peaceful practice.

2. Body scanning

A different way to relax and achieve a calm physical state is through body scanning. Just as we are rarely mindful of our breathing, unless we are having breathing problems, we also spend most of our time ignoring what's going on in our bodies. Our attitude when practicing body scanning is the exact opposite.

My teacher sometimes likens the desired attitude to that of a keen botanist, ornithologist, or suchlike setting off on an adventure in search of a particularly rare specimen. What on earth will we find? What are we about to notice that we have never noticed before? Will we be surprised by what has, hitherto, completely escaped our attention?

Starting at the crown of your head, focus all your attention on what you feel or don't feel there. This is not a flying visit. Take your time, like the ornithologists in their hideout, waiting to see if there's something going on which you've never really bothered to observe. The gentle rhythm of your pulse, perhaps? A tightness or slight itchiness of your scalp?

Whatever you find, simply continue to observe without any discursive thought or action. Observing the crown of your head is not a cue to launch into speculation about shampoo brands or hair growth products; it is just observation. Pure presence.

If you don't find anything, that's okay too. Next shift the focus of your attention down to your face. Your forehead—tight or relaxed? The feel of your closed eyelids. Your cheeks—warm, cool, or neither? The feel of your lips closed on each other. The sensation of air as it exhales from your nostrils and passes over your top lip. Notice any warmth, pulsing, numbness, moisture, sensitivity, pain. No detail should be too small to escape your attention. Your focus should be forensic.

I won't go into every detail of what you may or may not observe as your scan progresses. By now you get the picture. Having scanned your crown and face, your focus passes progressively through your head, neck, shoulders (often a place of trapped tension), one arm then the other, body, internal organs (tricky, but sometimes we detect something), one leg top to bottom, then the other. Then body scan your way back in the exact reverse order as slowly or quickly as you choose.

A variation of body scanning is to deliberately tighten, then relax, each muscle group as you work your way from head to toe. The warm surge as you release each muscle group can significantly add to the feeling of relaxation that accompanies this meditation.

How it feels: Just as with the two breath-based meditations, body scanning is a mindfulness practice as it applies to our physical being. The effect of focusing systematically on each part of the body is usually to make us feel thoroughly relaxed, especially if we build in the muscle tensing/releasing exercise. Body scanning can also produce some genuinely interesting findings when we notice aspects of our physicality we never noticed before. I personally find this one of the easiest meditations for concentration, possibly because while the focus remains turned on, the object of the focus continues to move. If you are forced to spend a long time in bed and/ or on your back, this is an especially appropriate meditation because muscle tightening/releasing is easier to achieve lying down than in a sitting posture.

The scanning process is one you can extend to last as long as you like, becoming a wonderful way to relax. But you can also become proficient in rapid scans, which will help you relax not only in your formal sessions, but during the day too.

One aftereffect of this practice is that we tend to become more mindful of our body and posture. If we practice body scanning regularly, our physical self-awareness develops during our off-cushion hours too. As office-bound ornithologists, or behind-the-wheel botanists, we begin to notice things about our body that we'd never observed before. Things that make us go . . . hmm!

3. WALKING MEDITATION

This form of meditation can be complementary to the calming effect of sitting, and a helpful way to energize your practice. First, plan your walking route. This could be as simple as walking around a room, or up and down the length of your house. If you opt for an outside location you'll need to find a level and interruption-free stretch of open ground.

Having set your route, begin in a standing position, with your arms hanging naturally at each side. If you wish, you can clasp your hands lightly in front of or behind you. I personally like to walk barefoot, weather permitting. Your gaze should rest, unfocused, a few yards in front of you at ground level, to help remove visual distractions. Before you move, do a quick body-scan, taking note of how your body feels, especially the muscles in your arms and legs. Then begin walking.

You can make the focus of your concentration "wide-angle" —that is, all the sensations you experience while you walk: the cool of wooden floorboards or tiles being replaced by the deep pile of a carpet, or the patterned strands of a seagrass floor covering. The subtly changing sounds as you progress. The scents associated with particular rooms or parts of a garden. Remember, your task is simply to note each sensation without further internal chatter, then let it go.

Alternatively, you can "zoom" your focus very specifically on the sensations of your feet touching the ground. Just as with breathing, the more you focus, the more detail you become aware of. The placement of the heel, before rolling the ball of the foot down on the floor. The pressing of the whole foot downward. The feeling on the ball of your foot and toes as you lift your foot off again.

It's interesting how self-conscious we become when we turn on our mindfulness. Rather like a child learning to ride a bicycle, who suddenly becomes aware they are perched on only two wheels, we may even feel a bit unstable. But just keep putting one foot in front of the other until you've completed a circuit, or the length of the planned route.

At that point, pause. If your mind has wandered, this provides a natural punctuation mark to bring your concentration back to the object of meditation, to remind yourself what you have chosen as your focus. Then begin again.

How it feels: Applying mindfulness to an activity you do all the time feels both natural but at the same time, paradoxically, strangely contrived. For most of us it has been a long time since we have given a thought to how we walk. The result, when you do, is quite curious. And it tends to last long after the practice finishes—at odd moments during the day you'll find yourself suddenly aware of lifting your foot off the ground in an action that's usually entirely beneath the radar of your awareness.

This is a pleasant, gentle meditation which allows for both "wide-angle" and "zoom" forms of mindfulness. Its dynamic nature makes it a good counterbalance to sitting. And it is also useful to help integrate mindfulness into everyday activities.

4. OBJECT-FOCUSED MEDITATION

THE MOMENT WE GIVE CLOSE ATTENTION TO ANYTHING, EVEN A BLADE OF GRASS, IT BECOMES A MYSTERIOUS, AWESOME, INDESCRIBABLY MAGNIFICENT WORLD IN ITSELF.
HENRY MILLER

Although all meditations have an object on which we focus, this practice refers to a specific physical item. It may be something we bring specifically for the purpose, such as an interesting seashell, crystal, or flower. Or we can simply make use of an available item, like a door handle or key. The object should be small enough that you can scrutinize it without having to move your head, and large enough to be able to look at comfortably without straining your eyesight.

It's useful to help stabilize the mind before you begin, perhaps with a few rounds of breath counting. Then, once your mind is more stable, open your eyes and study the chosen object.

Just as in the previous meditations, our purpose is to apply single-pointed concentration to the object. You may choose to gaze at it in its entirety, or apply a scanning technique where you start at one end and move very slowly to the other. The point is to observe every detail of the object in a nondiscursive way. The way the light falls on it, changes in texture or color from one part of the object to another, the lines of its edges and surfaces.

Most of us are in a hurry most of the time and, unless it is part of our job, we rarely pause to scrutinize an item in extreme detail. The commercial realities of the world in which we live mean that we are surrounded by stimuli competing for our attention. The ranting hysteria of retail advertising on radio and TV, and crazily flashing website advertisements, seem based on the depressing assumption that we have the attention spans of gnats.

This practice is a direct antidote to our usual fragmented observation. And when we do deliberately pause and look, it's amazing what richness we find. As Henry Miller observed, we can find interest and even pleasure in the most mundane objects when we choose to focus our attention on them.

There's a word which particularly comes to mind with this practice—the "thingness" of things. The word doesn't appear in the dictionary, but it refers to the intrinsic nature of something. The shellness of a shell. The keyness of a key. Not a quality we notice in our usual "on the run" mode. But when we slow right down, turn down the internal monologue as far as we're able, and focus our attention simply, mindfully, and nonjudgmentally, the simplest objects acquire an altogether different significance.

How it feels: Another gentle meditation, using an object as your focus, feels quite normal as we're used to scrutinizing things—just not in quite such detail. This is a less dynamic meditation than the previous ones, and it can be hard work to keep your attention fixed to the object. The reward is not only a deeper appreciation of the object itself during meditation, but revelations of the "thingness" of other things in moments after the meditation. This is especially true if you practice this meditation regularly. Just as mindfulness of walking can bring awareness of our bodies to us at unexpected moments, so mindfulness of an external object often enriches our appreciation of even quite ordinary things as we go about our daily lives. We may be sitting at our desk, staring at an everyday object we've looked at a thousand times before, when suddenly we're struck by something we've never noticed about it before. We begin to see the world in a more vivid and particular way, as though through new eyes.

5. Visualization

Visualization meditations are among the most powerful tools we have available to effect personal change. I sometimes think the word "visualization" is too restrictive, because the visual is not the only sense we should try to bring to our imagined or "visualized" activity. If you can evoke a tangible physical feeling, a sense of presence, if relevant even a fragrance or sound, so much the better. The more intensity you can create, using your full sensory repertoire, the better.

Visualizations are extremely flexible and can be developed and applied to deal with a range of physical and psychological needs. They are certainly an important part of healing meditation.

If you are wishing to achieve a greater level of calm in your everyday experience, or feel the need for a big boost of confidence to help with studies or an exam, if you are seeking greater self-assurance to deal with an expected bruising personal encounter, if you are tired of being depressed about your life or worried about money, if you want to feel more energetic, if . . . the possibilities are infinite. Whatever your personal needs, visualization provides a powerful method to create major change.

The cocoon

By way of an example, let's use a visualization favorite, the cocoon, with the objective of releasing stress and creating a state of calm radiance. Begin with a few rounds of breath-counting meditation. This is both to help settle your mind and to set things up for what follows.

Now visualize that you are surrounded by a cocoon of radiant white light. The feeling tone of the light is one of intense serenity and bliss. As you continue breathing, use each in-breath to imagine you are breathing in the brilliant light. With every inhalation, feel the light being drawn down into your body, and with it, the tranquility and happiness of the white light. Don't rush this.

Breath by breath, simply absorb more and more of the radiant serenity, feeling it permeate your entire body, washing through every organ, penetrating every cell, suffusing every atom of your being until you are completely absorbed in blissful white light. You can do this in a systematic way if you like, working from head to toe. Or, if you prefer, simply allow the white light to percolate through your body until there isn't an atom of your being that is not permeated with peaceful white light. Your breath will probably slow down as you do this—which is absolutely fine.

Once you have stabilized the strong sense that your whole body is now in the nature of light-filled serenity and bliss, remain absorbed in this state until the end of your session. By the time you wrap up by restating your motivation, you should be feeling significantly more relaxed, less pressured, and free from stress. You may even open your eyes with a smile on your face!

Like all visualizations, you can apply infinite variations to this one. If you have a strong sense of being burdened by a problem or emotion, you may, for example, choose to exhale this negativity in the form of thick black smoke. You are therefore not only absorbing positive energy, but also getting rid of the negative. Alternatively, you can visualize the negativity as black liquid being forced to leave your body through the pores and orifices of your lower body and being instantly absorbed into the ground.

The example above is the cocoon visualization as applied to stress reduction, but you can use the visualization to access whatever resources you need. Harmony, happiness, optimism, energy: you can use the same method and perhaps change the color of the light if this works better for you. Yellow/gold is an archetype many of us associate with happiness, wealth, and abundance, and green with harmony (radio and TV stations tend to put visiting guests in a "green room" to calm them down before being grilled). Various shades of blue are usually associated with healing, wholeness, and serenity, while red or orange is associated with energy and power.

These colors are mentioned only by way of suggestion. It is important that you personalize this practice using the colors and variations to achieve the outcomes that suit you best. If you are feeling depressed, and your idea of upliftment and energy is purple light with pink polka dots running through it, by all means use this. It can't be emphasized enough that you should use the colors and the qualities that are personally meaningful to you to get the most out of this practice.

How does visualization work? While scientific data on this will probably take some time to emerge, in overall terms my understanding is that our minds don't always differentiate between what is real and what is imagined. Our "fight–flight" mechanism will respond in exactly the same way if we come across a snake on the path, or a piece of hose we believe to be a snake. Sexual arousal can be stimulated by an imagined fantasy just as by the physical presence of our partner. The things that cause us to lose sleep in the middle of the night are as likely, if not more likely, to be imagined horrors, rather than something which is actually happening.

In short, most of us have quite powerful imaginations, and if we are able to vividly create an imagined state in which we receive certain qualities, our body–mind system responds as though we actually have, much like the placebo effect. Through visualization, we have the opportunity to make the imagined real.

It is also true that our minds are far more powerful and complex than we generally consider. Not only do our brains control a powerful, finely tuned, 24/7 pharmacology production facility, but beneath the threshold of our consciousness are experiences and abilities which we are able to access while in a relaxed, meditative state. Visualization provides a helpful and direct pathway to these powerful resources.

Another reason that visualization works has to do with the power of suggestion. If we suggest to ourselves that we have certain emotional or physical experiences of the world, and if that suggestion is powerful enough, we can also help the imagined become real. This is one reason that the motivation with which we begin a meditation session is so important. When we suggest something to ourselves repeatedly while we're feeling relaxed, over a period of time we are, in a sense, programming ourselves to carry through a suggestion.

To use an example of my own, one of the affirmations I've been using for some years is, "I am bursting with energy and robust good health." As anyone who knew me at school or early adulthood will confirm, I've never been a particularly athletic, high-energy individual, much preferring more cerebral, artistic pursuits. These days, however, I've become a regular gym bunny, going to Body Pump classes three times a week and sometimes more. I've never been so fit and healthy. I've been instructed by some of the best personal trainers in the business, and have a doctor who embraces complementary healthcare. I take fish oil and other supplements every morning, try to drink lots of water, regularly give my feet reflexology massages, and when I go away I really do miss my workouts. How on earth did this happen?

I can't prove anything, of course, but I believe my experience merely reflects a much broader trend that suggesting, visualizing, and imagining ourselves to exist in a particular way stimulates behaviors both consciously and below the level of our conscious mind which work to transform vision into reality. As we think, so we are. As we imagine, so we become.

From time to time high-profile books appear on the subject of how to use "spiritual" forces to achieve greater wealth, happier relationships, or other material benefits. Very often these will recommend motivations/affirmations along the lines I have outlined in this book, as well as detailed visualizations. For example, if one wants to move to a nicer home in a better suburb, one should cut out a photo of such a house and use it as the basis for visualization. Ditto the car—a specific make and model should be visualized, not just some generic image.

While I am not aware that any of these methods for material self-improvement have been subjected to proper scrutiny using, for example, control and test samples and rigorous analysis, there certainly seems to be extraordinary anecdotal evidence that the method can work. Whether the reported successes can be explained purely in terms of goal-setting, suggestion, and the use of visualization, or attributed to the mysterious energies of the universe, is a question yet to be answered.

To me what's more important is the power that visualization

has to shape our *perceptions* of reality. As already discussed in Chapter 3, one of the most powerful psychological benefits of meditation, which has been scientifically established, is its repositioning of our default "set point" for happiness. Yes, we may be able to use visualization to rearrange the externals of our lives, and that's no bad thing. But there are plenty of people living in fancy houses and driving wonderful new cars who are far from happy. Pleasure vs. happiness: we shouldn't forget the difference. How much more exciting is the opportunity to transform the way we experience reality, whatever our material circumstances? To enhance our day-to-day happiness, our sense of being part of a much more panoramic experience, and to develop a deep-down sense of well-being?

RELIGIOUS VISUALIZATION

Visualization is ideally suited to religious practice, and is used by the major contemplative traditions for just this reason. In an introductory book of this kind it isn't possible to provide anything near the level of detail that this subject deserves. But typically a deity or iconic figure such as Jesus, Mary, or Buddha is visualized at about forehead level a short distance in front of the meditator. Different-colored light or representative symbols are visualized radiating from the heart of the figure and absorbing into the body of the meditator, along with the transmission of qualities such as purification, peacefulness, healing, and power.

I would strongly recommend any reader with a keen interest in developing religious visualization practice to find a teacher in their relevant tradition to provide personal guidance. Apart from being given detailed visual instruction, it is probable you'll also be given relevant prayers and/or mantras to be recited, all adding to the totality of the experience of seeking oneness with the divine, or with ultimate reality, or at least with certain transcendental qualities.

How it feels: The infinite variety of visualizations means that there is no "typical" visualization experience—each will reflect the specific practice used and outcomes sought, whether they are greater peacefulness, energy, self-confidence, or bliss.

My experience, and that of other meditators I know, is that visualization enables an *intensity* of feeling which can be very enjoyable, as well as extremely useful. The degree to which you feel this will depend on your familiarity with the practice, as well as your own imaginative powers and concentration. Even if you feel woefully lacking in the imagination department, please persist. Visualization may feel gentle and relaxing, but it's used by goal-driven individuals in sports and business for good reason: it really works.

6. MINDFULNESS OF MIND

In the practices described so far, we've looked at using, as the object of your meditation, your breath, your body, an external object, and a visualization. What happens when you turn the spotlight of your attention to the mind itself?

This may seem a challenging meditation—and it is! Unlike the breath, the mind is a very subtle object of meditation. I remember all the questions I had when I started this particular practice. To begin with, having never deliberately tried to "find" my mind before, I wasn't entirely sure what I was look-ing for. What did it feel like? How did you know when you were watching it? How did you stop it slipping away from you once you had found it? Even more fundamentally, what *is* the mind? Perhaps the last question is what makes this, for me, such an amazing practice because once I developed some familiarity with it, I realized that for the first time in my life I had direct, live, real-time access to my mind.

Don't we have that all the time? Of course, but usually it's so obscured by thoughts, concepts, and mental abstractions that what we see is not the mind so much as what occupies it. Rather like living in permanently overcast conditions, we're so used to seeing clouds when we look up that we might mis-take the constant, oppressive weight of them for the sky. The nature of the mind is particularly well defined by Tibetan Bud-dhist teacher Sogyal Rinpoche: "Mind is like a crystal. Just as a crystal adopts the color of whatever surface you place it on, the mind will become just whatever we allow to occupy it."

To begin mindfulness of mind practice, a few rounds of breath meditation are important to stabilize the mind. Once you're feeling more focused and quiet, gently let go of the breath as the object of meditation. At first this feels very strange, as though without the breath to hold on to you're now in limbo. But just relax!

You probably won't have to wait long before the first thought pops up. Instead of engaging with it, as we usually do, try to take a more objective stance. As a thought emerges you can label it "this is a thought" before letting go of it. Or, if it helps, you can provide a somewhat more detailed label—"this is a thought about the future," "this is a thought about the past," or "this is a fantasy," and let the thought go. This process of labeling every thought as past, future, or fantasy can be very useful, especially at the beginning of our practice, as it helps us manage the agitation in our mind.

If you're anything like I was, when you begin you'll have precious little time from one thought to another to find out what there is between them. You will also find it a challenge not to get caught up in the content of the thoughts.

Speaking to other meditators, I know that while many find this practice very difficult to begin with, others take to it with the greatest of ease. I don't want to prejudice your likely experience of it, except to say that even if you do find it hard, it is very well worth persisting. I personally found this the toughest meditation practice of all when I started, but it is by far and away my favorite now.

Why? Because gradually we discover larger spaces between our thoughts. We become more aware that thoughts really are like clouds, passing through the vast spaciousness of mind. That our thoughts are not our mind, they are only passing fragments of mental activity. By using both mindfulness and awareness, we gradually do get better and better at letting go of thoughts and abiding in the relaxing peacefulness between them.

How it feels: In our usual mental state, this meditation doesn't feel much different from sitting with our thoughts—except that from time to time we remember what we're supposed to be doing and become painfully aware of just how agitated our minds really are! But if we're able to let the mental sediment settle, we start to experience a sense of space, peace, and light which is profoundly calming. It's hard finding the words to describe this feeling except as an awareness of coming home to oneself.

The quality of our pristine mind, while a source of happiness, is not a static experience. Meditators far more advanced than I report that dampening down the agitation and removing some of the obscuration is only the start of our positive experience, not the end point. To a more limited extent, my ability with the practice continues to improve incrementally, and even though I am no meditation champion, I have discovered nothing to rival this practice for providing a deeper sense of peaceful reassurance, especially in the face of any adversity in life. For when we are able to abide in this state, even if only for a few brief minutes, we see, directly, that our thoughts have no permanence. Where do they come from? Where do they go to? What is their nature?

When we can abide momentarily in the nature of our primordial mind, we become aware that whatever storms may be raging on the surface of our lives, they have no significance at all to our true nature, just as the darkest storm clouds cannot stain the sky.

It is also intriguing to ask, Who is the "I" that is watching my mind? Because the "I" we usually think of as being "me" has been unmasked as nothing more than a collection of thoughts—which have no substance and are constantly changing—who or what exactly are we left with?

I'd like to leave you to explore these ideas for yourself, both in formal meditation and afterwards. For further illumination on who the "I'" is that is watching the mind, please turn to Chapter 10: "A Bigger Picture."

7. Analytical/contemplative meditation

Analytical meditation is different from other forms in that it combines certain aspects of discursive thinking with single-pointed concentration. The purpose of the practice is to deepen our understanding of a particular truth and thereby enhance our self-awareness and opportunity for personal growth.

It is sometimes the case that while we accept an idea on an intellectual level, our behavior shows that we haven't fully internalized this truth—that is, we don't act in accord with our stated beliefs. A female friend of mine, for example, had a high degree of intellectual understanding that she was always attracted to the wrong kind of men. As a "rescuer" she had an unerring instinct to pick out the guy at the party who was enmeshed in a complex web of emotional and financial difficulties, before she embarked on a tortuous relationship whose painful ending was somehow inevitable right from the beginning. In another case, a male friend is quite willing to admit that he has a similarly self-destructive attraction to women who will replay the difficult relationship he endured as a child with his mother.

In both cases, intellectual recognition alone has not been enough to change behavior. It is only my female friend, who has undertaken analysis—fully exploring the subject at a profound level—who has been able to move on. She has now reached the point where men in need of rescue are no longer the irresistible attraction they once were.

In Buddhism, the word "realization" is used a fair bit when talking about the desired result of analytical meditation. Asking my teacher for a definition of a realization, he said it was when we reached an understanding of a particular truth which changed our behavior, be that a mental or behavioral change. Another way of putting it might be that our thoughts and actions become more congruent. Once we subjectively know something to be true, deep down, how can we consistently act as though it isn't?

Analytical meditation is therefore about developing a more profound appreciation of a particular subject or theme. It is not aimed at brainstorming ideas or coming up with arguments for and against a particular proposition. While both of these can be useful activities, they have no place in this particular practice.

To illustrate an analytical approach, most of us have some awareness that we are lucky to be living in a free and functioning democracy. We may sometimes refer to this when we talk with other people, or reflect on it ourselves, but in our usual hurried mode, we probably give as much attention to our good fortune as we do to our breathing, the feelings in our bodies, or the appearance of a brass doorknob—that is, very little.

Through analytical meditation we focus our thoughts very deliberately on a specific subject, usually reflecting on several related aspects of the subject, before arriving at a concluding thought and holding it in our mind single-pointedly. For example, an analytical meditation on the subject of our good fortune to be living in a democracy might consider the following points:

- I live freely in a stable democracy
- This society is tolerant and affluent
- I am not physically and/or mentally disabled
- I have access to whatever teachers, wisdom, or knowledge I wish to pursue
- The conditions of a human life don't get any better

We explore the significance of each point, one at a time, before moving on to the next one. For example, for the first point we might consider how the vast majority of people on planet Earth do not enjoy most of the freedoms we take for granted. What is it really like waking up in the morning in a hotbed of armed violence or instability, like so many parts of Africa, South America, and the Middle East? Explore this idea and try to imagine the reality of other, very different lives. What must it be like being born in a persecuted ethnic, political, or social group, taught to hate or fear some other group from the moment we are conscious?

Moving on to the next point, we might ask the same kinds of questions about societies which exist in grinding poverty. Over a third of the world's population lives on less than $2 a day, something we tend to forget when we open the paper every morning and find ourselves looking longingly at advertisements for the latest Mercedes Benz. What would it be like to live on so little money? Not just for a few days, or even weeks, but relentlessly, year in, year out, with little prospect of change? What must it be like to know you could have saved your child from sickness or even death, but couldn't afford the $5 vaccination? Considering the day-to-day lives of people who share exactly the same hopes and fears that we do, but have little prospect of enjoying even the most limited financial security, what sort of position does that put us in? And so on.

We make our way through the analysis, contemplating the significance of each point before arriving at the conclusion: that the conditions in which we are living really don't get much better. We are among the top few percentiles of the luckiest people in the world. Motivated by the analysis we have just undertaken, we hold this thought single-pointedly for several minutes.

How it feels: It is difficult to articulate the power of this meditation until we have tried it. The usual response is a far more profound appreciation of the subject of our choice—in this case our immense good fortune—which in turn provides a much better perspective on whatever difficulties we may be experiencing.

Analytical meditation is a particularly useful technique to apply when we're feeling bored or lacking in motivation to do something useful—be that at work, home, or in the area of self-development. Meditating on truths such as the free society in which we live, change and impermanence, our brief lives and certain death, all help develop a more fully realized understanding that, compared to most human beings with whom we share the planet I, the writer of this book, and you, the reader, already live like princes and have privileges and opportunities available to us which are unbelievably precious and rare. Developing a sense of appreciation of this is a truly life-enhancing experience.

8. Meditating with a mantra

Meditating with a mantra is probably the most common form of meditation there is. It is widely practiced across the world's major religions and is also the basis for what is probably the largest secular form of meditation—Transcendental Meditation.

In using mantra, the object is a short phrase repeated over and over, often counted with the aid of rosary beads or beads known by their Sanskrit name, *mala*. At one level it is difficult to make any generalizations about the practice because it is understood so differently by its varied practitioners. For example, some traditions understand that the purpose of the practice is to penetrate deeply into the meaning of the mantra. Others say the meaning of the mantra is, in itself, not so important—the simple repetition of certain specific words or phrases has a particular power. According to one school of thought, the vibrations on the upper palate caused by sound and tongue have a profound effect on the body's energy system. Yet others say that there's nothing particularly magical about specific syllables: the impact of any repeated phrase is enough to free the mind from its perpetual busyness and help create a more expansive mind.

There are also different theories about how mantra works. Is it, as some say, the impact of a repeated sound on one's brain and central nervous system? Listening to Gregorian or Tibetan monastic chanting, it's easy to see how such a conclusion might be reached—except that in daily practice mantras are mostly whispered under the breath. Some of the more esoteric traditions talk about how mantra impacts on the subtle energy flow within our bodies.

It's also true that mantra is used quite differently by different traditions. Some focus purely on a mantra as the sole object of meditation. Others use mantra more to provide the "soundtrack" for visualizations of varying degrees of complexity. None of these widely disparate views should, however, deter us from this practice because, at a more important level, the simple fact is that mantra meditation is powerfully effective.

Because Transcendental Meditation is widely practiced in the US, TM meditators have been the subjects of over six hundred research studies into the effects of meditation, some of which are quoted in this book. The positive impact of mantra practice on physical and mental well-being has therefore been repeatedly verified by research. It's also the case that some of the research carried out by Dr. Richard Davidson, mentioned in Chapter 3, studied a number of advanced Tibetan Buddhist practitioners, who used mantra as a core practice in long-term retreats.

Mantra meditation used according to a number of different traditions has shown itself to be highly effective at stimulating positive change. Which is why the specifics of how and why mantra works are, to me, of less interest than the simple truth that it does.

Instructions for mantra meditation are very simple. Close your eyes and concentrate on a mantra, repeating it in barely a whisper. You should be aware of the sound of it, but no one else should. It helps to continue the mantra on both the in- and out-breath, creating a continuous flow on which to focus.

Most of the best-known mantras are specifically religious. Among Tibetan Buddhists, the best-known mantra is "Om mani pedme hum" (pronounced "Om muni péma hung" and translated as "Hail to the jewel in the lotus"—a phrase with multiple meanings). In the Christian tradition, the Saint Francis mantra is "My God and my All," and the Jesus prayer, practiced in Eastern churches for about 1600 years, is "Lord Jesus Christ, Son of God, have mercy on me a sinner." Hare Krishna devotees use "Hare Krishna Hare Krishna, Krishna Krishna Hare Hare."

TM provides practitioners with their own mantras, though the method by which they do this is a closely guarded secret. Neurolinguistic programmers recommend that we make up our own mantra as a form of affirmation to implant in our subconscious mind—such as, "I am healthy, attractive, and enjoy effortless abundance." I've also come across the telephone directory approach to mantra creation, which is to randomly keep opening a phone book, point at names, and use the first syllable in each case to build up a mantra of predetermined length. I mention this only in passing. Call me old-fashioned, but I couldn't bring myself to spend hours every week repeating "Wongsmith Blackstein."

My firm recommendation to meditation newcomers would be to put mantra recitation to one side while you get started on other practices, especially breath-based meditations. I wanted to cover it as one of the major types of meditation in this chapter, because not to do so would be a glaring omission.

But for the reasons already outlined, it would be much better to receive direct guidance, as well as a mantra, from an expert in the tradition of your choice, be that secular or religious.

How it feels: Once we become familiar with a particular mantra, it provides a very clear object of meditation. Repeating it becomes automatic very quickly. This can provide a reassuring rhythm to our meditation. And, if we choose to continue the meditation after ending mantra recitation, the inner quiet that follows feels wonderfully peaceful and expansive.

Just as in other forms of meditation, the impact of mantra continues off-cushion when we recollect the mantra at intervals during the day and reexperience the relaxed qualities which accompanied it. We can deliberately evoke these pleasant feelings at any moment by verbally, or only mentally, repeating the mantra. In this sense the words of the mantra assume a deeply felt significance which is individual to each meditator.

CHAPTER SIX

Seven Ways to Turbocharge Your Meditation

~~~~~~

I BELIEVE THAT CONSTANT EFFORT, TIRELESS EFFORT, PURSUING CLEAR
GOALS WITH SINCERE EFFORT IS THE ONLY WAY.
THE DALAI LAMA

1. MAKE IT PART OF YOUR DAILY ROUTINE

MY TEACHER often likens meditation practice to a river flowing through our life. In the early stages, like a mountain spring, our practice is fleeting and undeveloped. There may be a fair few leaps and crashes before we settle into a more regular rhythm. Little by little our practice continues to grow and mature until eventually it becomes like a vast river, attracting everything else to it, no longer a small trickle in our life, but the most compelling force of it. The river may still encounter obstacles, but they are of little consequence. It will simply flow over or around them, having developed a smooth, calm, but unstoppable momentum.

It's a wonderful metaphor and an entirely appropriate one, judging from both my own personal experience as well as my observation of much more advanced meditators. The question is, How do we get from the Andes Mountains to the mouth of the Amazon? How do we develop our own meditation into a calm and steady flow of unstoppable power? "Through regular practice" is the simple, unspectacular answer. As much as we might wish for a short cut to the blissful state of a mind untroubled by anything it encounters, the reality is that such a mind arises only as a result of regular practice over a long period of time.

An instructive story describes how the revered Tibetan teacher Marpa, saying goodbye to his student Milarepa, whom he'd taught for many years, told him that he'd saved his most precious teaching until last. If Milarepa wished to achieve great insight, he said, he should observe carefully. Turning round, Marpa dropped his pants to show his student the calluses that had formed on his backside from all the hours he had spent meditating. With our fleece-filled meditation cushions and foam rubber mats, modern-day meditators may not need to develop butts like rhinoceroses, but the point still stands: if we want to get anything out of meditation, we need to make it a regular part of our life.

When you start, it is much better to do just a few minutes every day than longer periods of meditation on a sporadic basis. A daily ten-minute session is much better than an hour on the weekend. What we're trying to create is a constant current that will begin to counterbalance the ongoing agitation we experience.

In Chapter 4 we looked at the when and where of meditation. Whatever works best for you, given your personal circumstances and temperament, the important thing is to do it regularly, preferably every day.

I would also recommend that you keep the session to a

length of time that feels comfortable. This is because in the early stages of meditation it's easy to become discouraged and have thoughts along the lines of: "This might work for other people, but I don't have the right personality/mind/lifestyle/partner for meditation." Or: "I've been doing this for six months and my concentration is no better than when I started." With thoughts like these, you may start to resent the time you spend meditating and consider giving up.

Much better to keep your practice light and easy to begin with; short sessions, and concentrated attention, especially towards the end of your practice so that you "finish like a winner" and feel encouraged for the next day. Better to end a short session thinking you could have gone on longer than keep glancing at your watch with the thought that has passed through the mind of every meditator at some stage—*My watch must have stopped. It's been longer than two minutes—surely?!*

Having reviewed the meditation practices outlined in the previous chapter, you may decide you quite like the sound of several of them. On what basis should they be practiced? My own preference is to have a simple calendar of activity so that, for example, Mondays, Wednesdays, and Fridays are breath-counting days; Tuesdays, Thursdays, and Saturdays are visualization days; and Sundays are for whatever I'm in the mood to do.

On this point, I once asked a high-ranking Tibetan lama which of a number of meditation practices I should focus on. He gave me an indulgent smile and said simply, "Whichever you enjoy the most." D'oh!

2. Practice with Equanimity

JUST BECAUSE YOU FIND SOMETHING DIFFICULT TO DO, DON'T THINK
THAT IT'S HUMANLY IMPOSSIBLE. IF SOMETHING IS HUMANLY POSSIBLE
AND APPROPRIATE, BELIEVE THAT IT CAN BE ATTAINED BY YOU.
MARCUS AURELIUS, EMPEROR OF ROME

Of all the factors determining our success as meditators, this is the single most important one. Most readers of this book are busy people who like to get things done. High achievers. Individuals eager to develop their full potential. So what happens when we sit on our meditation cushion and discover that we can't concentrate for even two minutes without gross agitation disturbing our focus? What happens when the same thing happens the following day . . . and the day after that?

If we're too outcome-focused in our attitude, we will swiftly conclude that meditation is too hard, or we're not suited to it, or some other such delusional garbage. Because the reality is that our experience is no worse than anyone else's sitting down for the first time, and it may even be a whole lot better.

The difference between those who stay with the practice and those who quit is one of attitude. Are we able to handle repeated frustration? Is our emotional intelligence sufficiently developed such that we can put up with short-term irritation in the interests of all the very great benefits reviewed in this book?

There is no shortage of useful advice on how to cultivate an attitude of equanimity. A meditation colleague once told me that, at the end of a session in which he'd caught his mind straying countless times, he'd congratulate himself for having so frequently caught it! After all, he explained, much better that than drifting off on some epic narrative ramble that only finished at the end of the session. Quite so!

I have also heard it said that we should feel grateful to the part of our mind that recognizes agitation, and enables us to do something about it. Slightly more stern practitioners suggest we should treat our rambling mind like a small child, leading it firmly, but gently, back to where we want it to be.

The way we choose to frame or reframe our experience of an agitated mind is a necessarily individual one. Some of the ways I deal with it personally are to reflect that a bad session, or even a week or a month of bad sessions, is of little consequence in the journey of a lifetime. I also remember that, even though I have felt distracted, scientific evidence shows that meditation still produces benefits. My time isn't being wasted. And I also liken meditation to the stock market: sure, there may be disappointing sessions ranging from lackluster to catastrophic, but in the long term, over a period of years, my meditation focus, like the stock market, can only go up.

What's more, after we have been meditating for a period of months or years, we know that just because we have a terrible session doesn't mean the next one isn't going to be wonderfully focused and calm. Equanimity evolves naturally out of experience.

3. Make sure it's relevant

While there are many good reasons to meditate, we should be clear about what we personally want to achieve. Stress reduction and inner peace? Self-confidence in our dealings with others? Healing from disease? Patience and anger management? Perhaps we are meditating for several different reasons. That's fine too—the important thing is to be quite clear about why we're engaging in the practice.

We can help ensure that meditation is relevant to us by creating a personalized and motivating statement, or objective, at the start of each session (see Chapter 4). The importance of this can't be exaggerated. To cultivate a regular, disciplined meditation practice is difficult with only a woolly idea of what we're setting out to achieve, and a vague understanding of how we might benefit. Given the obstacles we will face along the way, we need to be focused on our outcomes and have confidence in the method we're using.

In the visualization section we discussed how creativity can be important to make a meditation personally relevant. But this overall principle extends beyond visualization practice to encompass the whole meditation context and session. For example, if you find that lighting a candle at the beginning of each meditation session is a useful way of inserting a "punctuation mark" into your life, and marking out this time period as one distinct from what went before and what follows later, by all means do this. I personally like to light a stick of Nag Champa incense when I meditate. At the time I light it, I follow the Tibetan Buddhist teaching of dedicating the session that follows to the benefit of all living beings. Why do I bother with the incense? Simply because I associate incense with qualities I'd like to cultivate—tranquility, transcendence, benevolence, a sense of the timelessness and unity of all things.

If decorating the place where you meditate with a few meaningful items helps, you should do this too. These could be religious icons of some kind, or they could be other objects. Albert Einstein once said, "The most beautiful and profound emotion that we can experience is the sensation of the mystical." Cultivating this sensation can be most enjoyable. I once went to visit a Tibetan Buddhist monk and was surprised to find in his meditation room, along with all the traditional wall-hangings and statues, a large collection of crystals. I'm not aware of any teachings on crystals in Buddhism, but that's not really the point. The monk, or perhaps his students, felt that the presence of the crystals would enhance their meditative experience. At some level their presence resonated with the purpose of this room. It helped mark out the time spent here as precious and not to be wasted.

4. Cultivate spot meditation

The meditation practices described so far in this book have mostly been of the formal variety. And even though our sessions may be brief, there is no substitute for setting aside time to cultivate our concentration, mindfulness, and awareness. But that doesn't mean we can't also "top off" our meditation experience with brief, or spot, meditations during the course of each day.

These do not involve taking our shoes off and assuming the seven-point meditation posture in the boardroom, on the train, or at the child care facility. Instead, it's more about using some of the between-jobs periods we have in our daily life to recollect and reexperience some of the inner peace or other qualities of our formal sessions.

There are moments in every day when we find ourselves having to wait. At the traffic lights. Beside the photocopier. In a meeting room. Outside the school. And while it may be that we use some of that waiting time planning our day, there's also a good chance we're not thinking of anything in particular. How much better would it be to use these moments to recollect a feeling of tranquility? To act as a circuit breaker to the way we're feeling if we're having a bad day? To help the stream of meditation running through our life develop into a full-flowing river?

At such moments it's helpful to briefly check your posture, relax back into your chair, unhunch your shoulders, take a deep breath and exhale slowly, recollecting your motivation as you do. These simple steps are, in themselves, extraordinary, in that we are self-consciously interrupting the usual pattern of our internal chatter. It's even better if you can follow up the exhalation with a few moments of meditation.

Breath-based meditation lends itself ideally to this practice. It's quite easy to focus on the breath while at the same time remaining aware of the color of the traffic lights, or continuing another routine activity. And it always surprises me what just one or two rounds of really focused breath counting can achieve in terms of relaxation. We may not end the practice feeling that the whole world has changed because of it, but do we feel better now than we did one or two minutes ago?

I use toilet breaks for spot meditation. They strike me as being ideal opportunities to reexperience my meditative purpose because they happen regularly throughout the day, I'm on my own, and I'm free to think what I like. Or to not think.

Since I've been doing this for some years, I'm now completely in the habit of conducting spot meditations half a dozen times a day or more. Interestingly, far from interrupting or detracting from my mental productivity, I've found that they have the opposite effect. Coming back to a challenge or difficult situation is always easier with a meditative break, however short, than without it.

Lavatory breaks may not suit everyone, and that's okay. The important thing is to find a way to bring the mind back to a relaxed state during the course of each day. If there are routine chores we can use for this purpose, transforming a humdrum activity into one of personal significance, how wonderful is that?

Is there a traffic light or a freeway on-ramp where you regularly find yourself stuck for minutes at a time? Hurrah! Instead of getting exasperated, making unnecessary cell phone calls, or listening to talk radio, why not use the time for some breath counting? Finding yourself at a lunch event having to listen to a speaker uttering the usual platitudes, why not spend a few minutes studying the table flowers in forensic detail in an object-focused meditation? Afterwards you can privately contrast your experience of vivid freshness and color with the groans of your fellow lunch guests!

Moment by moment as we capture control of our thinking time, we are better able to influence our mental destiny. Remind ourselves of our meditative purpose. Evolve from mountain spring to majestic river.

5. Develop off-cushion mindfulness

REALIZE DEEPLY THAT THE PRESENT MOMENT IS ALL YOU EVER HAVE.
ECKHART TOLLE

Most of us have no difficulty listing our favorite drinks. The cappuccino from our local café. The cabernet from our preferred vineyard. Our personal number-one brand of beer. During the course of any given year, how many hundreds of combined gallons of all these do we drink? But of the total gallons consumed, how many drinks do we ever really consciously enjoy?

Sitting down at the local coffee shop with the morning coffee and newspapers, how often do we find ourselves so engrossed in that day's stories of murder and mayhem, property prices or stock market reports, that before we know it our cup of premium-priced coffee is almost empty and we only fully appreciated the first mouthful. Settling down to a nice chilled glass of white wine at dusk, do we drink the wine mindfully, relishing each mouthful, or does that usually apply to just the first few sips, before we're caught up in conversation, television, or organizing the family?

And these are activities we supposedly enjoy—things that supposedly give us pleasure! What about all the rest of our time? All the hours we spend attending to the basic logistics of our lives, getting from A to B, carrying out routine tasks, or occupied in leisure time? The awkward reality is that much of our activity is surprisingly mindless.

We might be driving to work on a beautiful spring morning, but in our minds we're already fighting our side of the 11:00 A.M. argument we're expecting with a colleague. Instead of making productive use of a quiet afternoon, we may spend hours mentally wrestling with how to deal with a client whose payment is now more than sixty days overdue. We may be somewhere, but our mad monkey is somewhere else, hollering and whooping, causing nothing but disquiet.

On-cushion mindfulness of meditation is one direct opponent to our mental agitation. But it's also useful to complement that experience by deliberately setting out to cultivate mindfulness of other activities. In the same way that spot meditation helps us extend the impact of our practice throughout the day, it's also useful to develop our off-cushion mindfulness if we wish to take back control of our thought processes, little by little, from the mad monkey.

Just as it's a good idea to identify moments in the day when it would be useful to cultivate spot meditation, we all have to undertake routine activities which provide an opportunity to practice mindfulness. In fact, applying mindfulness to some of our least-liked chores can be a highly effective way to make them a lot more interesting.

I've yet to meet the person who says they actually enjoy washing dishes—or, for that matter, stacking the dishwasher—but it's an interesting transformative technique to say to ourselves, Next time I have to tidy the kitchen and stack the dishwasher, I'm going to treat it as an experiment in mindfulness. Instead of resenting the waste of leisure time, I'm going to turn it into a high-quality meditative experience. Even the mere thought of doing this can change our attitude to doing the dishes and, in a small but significant way, help us find greater meaning in the things we have to do.

Next time the dishes need to be cleared up, apply mindfulness as already described in this book. Instead of trying to reconcile your credit card statement in your head, or work out who is doing what next Saturday, focus complete attention on the smooth, substantial feeling of the plates in your hands. Notice the curve of the forks, the design of their handles; really concentrate on the fragrance of the dishwashing liquid. Perhaps notice beauty in the same dinnerware set you've used, unseeing, for the past five years. You will have an intensity of experience you've never associated with dishwashing or kitchen cleaning before. You may even, to your surprise, derive an unexpected pleasure from it—not that you're going to admit this to anyone!

At first, applying mindfulness to a humdrum task may seem contrived or artificial, though you shouldn't let that bother you. For as you'll have gathered, by using different methods of mindfulness skillfully in different contexts throughout the day, we're able to start shifting the balance of our mental activity from less to more mindful.

The mad monkey is still there, but forced behind an ever-widening perimeter. As the quality of our mindfulness improves, so does our ability to make the changes described in Chapter 3 on psychological benefits—particularly living in the present and replacing negative attitudes with positive ones.

Along with these, we discover other life-enhancing experiences in formal practice, including a much greater capacity to experience inner peace and an expanded sense of connectedness with others. We find ourselves wishing for the day when our every waking moment can become a meditation.

One of the stories I like best of all tells how the novice monk asks a revered and ancient lama, "What's it like to be an enlightened being?" To which the lama replied after a moment, "I walk and I eat and I sleep." The young novice was startled by the simplicity of his answer. "But I also walk and eat and sleep," he said. "Yes," smiled the lama. "When I walk, I walk. When I eat, I eat. And when I sleep, I sleep."

6. Remember the Major Benefits of Minor Changes

It's almost always hard work when we start to meditate. If you don't find this, perhaps you should make an appointment with the Dalai Lama to find out which highly realized yogi you were in a previous lifetime! Seriously, finding ourselves confronted, perhaps for the first time in our lives, with the reality of our agitated minds, it's easy to get the feeling that our efforts are futile. That no matter what we do, the scale of the problem is just so overwhelming we might just as well give up.

If you share any of these feelings, my first suggestion is— relax! You're not alone. Not only is your reaction entirely normal, in some ways it would be concerning if you *didn't* have these feelings, and instead believed yourself to be a mere hop, skip, and a jump away from perfect concentration. It's also worth remembering that, although we may not feel like we're making much progress in our sessions, even subtle changes can have a marked impact on our lives.

A nutritionist recently told me that when seriously overweight people with very bad eating habits sought her advice, she knew she could help them achieve much more dramatic weight loss with only small changes to their diet compared to people who were less overweight with better diets. This was because their eating habits were so bad that all it took was a couple of changes to achieve dramatic results.

A woman who switched from drinking ten regular soft drinks per day to ten zero-calorie versions might not feel she was making much of a change, but all of a sudden she would be ingesting the equivalent of about one hundred teaspoons of sugar less *per day*. By contrast, a woman who usually drank only two zero-calorie cans each day would have to make far more radical changes to her regime to have anything near this kind of impact.

In much the same way, we may not feel that a mere ten or fifteen minutes of daily low-grade meditation is achieving very much—and if we were highly accomplished yogis, we would be right. But let's be honest about the state of the mind we are starting out with! Like the overweight woman who has been drinking high-calorie soft drinks for years, we too have done nothing about our extreme mental agitation. Is it really surprising we can't even count ten breaths?

The start of a regular meditation routine, however, marks a turning point every bit as dramatic as the switch to zero-calorie drinks. Even though we may not feel we're doing a lot, the effect on our mental continuum is dramatic. And the longer we stay with it, the more self-evident the effect. What's more, just as the now somewhat less overweight woman may feel encouraged by her initial weight loss to cut down on her daily serving of fries, we may also wish to supplement our formal, sitting practice with spot meditations throughout the day, or the regular recollection of mindfulness. We have embarked on a journey from which we have no wish to return to our previous less-enlightened state.

During the course of that journey, especially in the early stages, it's very useful to remember the benefits of meditation, as summarized in the early chapters of this book. It's quite possible to go for months without feeling we are making any progress and, depending on what else is going on in our lives, we may even believe that the sacrifice of our time just isn't worth it. Wouldn't an extra fifteen minutes in bed achieve just as much?

If and when you feel this way, skim through the benefits. Focus on those with the greatest appeal to you. Ask yourself if the alternative uses of your time really are of more importance. In a year's time, will you wish you had continued with your practice, or agree that those extra minutes in bed each day were just as valuable? What about in five or ten years' time? Who knows where the journey could have taken you by then?

7. Find a teacher and support group

This book is intended to provide everything you need to start the regular practice of meditation. For the first four years of my own practice I did nothing but breath counting, and in retrospect that foundation was very useful. However, my meditation practice was only really turbocharged once I found a regular teacher and support group.

In my own case, this took the form of the Tibetan Buddhist Society in Perth, Australia, but it's important to say, very quickly, that I'm not advocating any particular religious or secular group to meditators. Such a choice is one that only you can make. What I would say about choosing a teacher or organization is that you should take your time, shop around, and find out as much as possible about the different options from current and former students. Just as most of us prefer personal recommendations for doctors, accountants, lawyers, personal trainers, or other service providers, exactly the same holds true of meditation teachers.

Once going to classes, you can make up your own mind. Does the teacher "walk the talk" or does he or she seem uptight, self-absorbed, or disorganized? Is this a person you can relate to, or do you simply live in different worlds? Are you able to feel inspired and motivated by this person? Do you respect them? It may take you a while to find the right person, or you may have the good fortune to encounter someone with whom you feel an immediate rapport. However long it takes, there are good reasons to seek out an expert, as well as kindred spirits following the same path as yourself.

The first, and perhaps most obvious, reason for this is that no book can respond to the challenges we encounter in meditation with the immediacy of a teacher. While I've tried to cover all the important instructions, benefits, and obstacles in this book, I also know from experience that it's much easier to ask a question in class than to plough through a book trying to figure out the answer to something which may not be directly addressed.

A teacher also performs an extremely helpful role in keeping us motivated and inspired. This is especially true if you are not surrounded by family members, friends, or colleagues who meditate and you are in effect going solo. During the course of any average week, when you are subject to the familiar bombardment of stress and negativity, it can come as something of a relief to step into a meditation class and be reminded of the different way of experiencing reality. Regular classes help reinforce the new paradigm: that what matters is not so much what's going on out there, as how we're experiencing it in our minds. With the right teacher, meditation classes are a wonderful reminder of the journey of transformation on which we have embarked. I regard my own weekly classes as being like free psychotherapy and almost always come away from them with a renewed sense of enthusiasm for my practice in particular, and life in general.

And why do I suggest it is worthwhile to share the experience with other meditation students? First of all, they help normalize our behavior. If we don't have much contact with others who are practicing meditation, when we start out we can easily form the mistaken view that we are doing this all on our own, that our activity is on the margins of society for good reason, and that we might just as well go with the flow of agitated consumerism like everyone else. Of course, if we walk into a meditation room full of loopy-looking people, we may take this as confirming our suspicions! But the reality is that there are many different organizations offering meditation classes, appealing to a wide variety of tastes. Finding the teacher and group that best suits us is our particular challenge.

Fellow students can also be a valuable source of information about our practice. It's quite usual to have lots of questions when we begin meditating, and even if we do have the opportunity to ask a teacher, we may not want to parade our ignorance in front of everyone in the group. By speaking to those who are just a bit further along the road than ourselves, we can often gain very useful suggestions as well as the motivation to help us keep going.

CHAPTER SEVEN

Measuring Progress

~~~~~~

BE PATIENT WITH EVERYONE, BUT ABOVE ALL WITH YOURSELF. I MEAN
DO NOT BE DISHEARTENED BY YOUR IMPERFECTIONS, BUT ALWAYS
RISE UP WITH FRESH COURAGE.
SAINT FRANCIS DE SALES

IN CHAPTER 3 we saw that when long-term meditators are monitored with fMRI scans and other equipment, the results of their sessions show brain activity patterns way in advance of novices. Having put in the hours, they achieve the results. Calmer, more robust, and significantly happier individuals, their personal transformation is not a subjective matter of opinion—it is scientifically measurable.

For the majority of us without ready access to fMRI equipment, how do we monitor the progress of our meditation practice? A useful yardstick for over two and a half thousand years has been "The Nine Levels of Meditative Concentration." Starting at Level 1, where we effectively spend more time being distracted than focusing on the object of meditation, each of the nine levels is outlined. By reviewing each level, we're able to gauge for ourselves which most accurately describes our own meditative experience.

But before we do, an important reminder about expectations management. One of the main challenges of meditating in the twenty-first century is that the process of subduing our minds does not accord with most of our usual timescales. If we are unfit and decide to join classes at a gym, within a few months of attending several sessions a week our cardiovascular performance will have dramatically improved. Most people take only months from the first time they sit behind a steering wheel until the day they become licensed drivers. If we decide that an MBA is the best way to advance our career, a single year of intensive study is what it will take to get the right piece of paper.

Making progress in meditation is, however, a much longer-term undertaking. Part of the reason for placing so much emphasis on suggestions such as practicing with equanimity, remembering the major benefits of minor changes, and managing our expectations is to offer different ways to counter our expectations that, for example, after six months of meditating we should be at least up to Level 4!

Probably the best advice on expectations management comes from the Dalai Lama: "Inner development comes step-by-step. You may think, 'Today my calmness, my mental peace, is very small,' but still, if you compare, if you look five, ten, or fifteen years back and think, 'What was my way of thinking then? How much inner peace did I have then and what is it today?' Comparing it with what it was then, you can realize that there is some progress, there is some value. This is how you should compare—not with today's feeling and yesterday's feeling, or last week or last month, even not last month, even not last year, but five years ago. Then you can realize what improvement has occurred internally. Progress comes by maintaining constant effort in daily practice."

THE NINE LEVELS OF MEDITATIVE CONCENTRATION

Level 1: Placing the mind

At this stage of your meditative practice, you spend more time during each session being distracted than you do focusing on the object of meditation. While you're able to place your mind on the object of meditation for short periods, you also become aware, perhaps for the first time, of the full extent of your mental agitation. There's only one way to go from here and it's up!

Level 2: Placement with continuity

While most of your meditation session is still distracted, you can sometimes hold the object of concentration for two minutes or more before being interrupted by gross agitation or dullness.

Level 3: Patchlike placement

The balance of your meditation sessions has changed so that the majority of your time is now spent engaged with your chosen object of meditation. Also, when you lose the object through distraction or dullness, you find it easier to resume concentration than you used to since your mindfulness is improving.

Level 4: Close placement

Your meditative concentration continues to improve to the point that while you still experience periods of agitation and/or dullness, you can now hold the object of meditation over longer periods of time—between five and ten minutes' duration.

Level 5: Controlling
You can now meditate for an entire session without your concentration being disrupted by gross agitation or dullness, but you still experience subtle agitation and/or dullness. Subtle dullness is the particular challenge.

Level 6: Pacifying
At this stage you are not only able to meditate for an entire session without your concentration being disturbed, you also experience only a small degree of subtle agitation and/or dullness. Subtle agitation is the particular challenge of this level.

Level 7: Complete pacification
Your concentration has improved to the point that if any subtle agitation or dullness arises, you are able to quickly overcome it through your greatly increased power of concentration.

Level 8: Single-pointed concentration
You are now able to hold the object of meditation completely throughout the whole session with only slight effort required at the start of the session.

Level 9: Placement with equanimity
In this final stage you are able to concentrate on an object of meditation for any length of time without effort.

CHAPTER EIGHT

Using Meditation to Heal

~~~~~~

MEDITATION IS THE SINGLE MOST POWERFUL TOOL TO AID RECOVERY
FROM DISEASE AND LEAD TO A LIFE OF MAXIMUM HEALTH.
IAN GAWLER, THE GAWLER FOUNDATION

M ANY PEOPLE come to meditation as a result of being diagnosed with a serious illness. This chapter is written for exactly such people. Given that various forms of cancer, as well as cardiovascular diseases, are the most feared killers in our society, many references in this chapter will be to people with those conditions. However, the powerful holistic effects of meditation apply across all disease categories, and if you are suffering from another illness, the same analysis and instruction that follow will almost certainly apply.

In this chapter we will look at how meditation helps treat disease. There are some simple, specific, and powerful meditations you can use right away. But first, to put all this in context, perhaps we need to answer the simple question: why do we get ill in the first place?

WHY WE GET ILL

The causes of diseases are so numerous and complex that, on one level, even attempting to answer such a question in a few paragraphs may seem crazy. We all know that there are inter-related genetic and environmental triggers for many illnesses, and that the significant research being undertaken in laboratories worldwide is constantly revealing new insights about the development and treatment of many diseases.

Not so long ago I asked a medical friend why a mutual acquaintance had been struck with cancer. He immediately launched into a detailed account of cancer cell growth, free radicals, the failure of the immune system, and other such factors. "That's not so much what I was after, Terry," I said, when he paused for breath. "That's more *how* she got cancer. I was thinking more along the lines of *why*?" "Why?" He seemed taken aback I should even be asking such a question, as though it was one of life's great imponderables.

Why is it that someone develops cancer at the age of sixty-five—why not three years before, ten years later, or, better still, not at all? Why is it that someone can be exposed to exactly the same virus on several occasions without any ill effect, but another time with deadly consequences?

"Why me?" is a question anyone suffering from a serious illness will naturally ask themselves. Perhaps I shouldn't have taken on so many responsibilities at work. Maybe I'm being punished for something I did in a previous lifetime. Is it because of the electricity pole running down the side of the house?

Some readers may believe, like my medical friend, that the "why?" question is a matter of pure conjecture: fate, karma, God, or plain bad luck—take your pick. Why does anything happen? And anyway, do the whys and wherefores really matter when we're stuck with an illness for which we urgently need help? But the "why" of disease is not a subject we should dismiss so easily. And far from being irrelevant, if we can go some way towards answering why something arose, perhaps that will also provide some useful suggestions on how to stop it getting worse, if not help us make a full recovery.

To answer the "why" of disease, it's helpful to reflect on the body–mind continuum described at the beginning of Chapter 2. There we looked at our tendency to see body and mind in dualistic terms. We say things like, "My arm was badly scraped from where I skidded across the asphalt, but I'm okay," as though the badly scraped arm is somehow separate from the "I" that is okay. Our default mode is to think of our minds as the masters, owners, or controllers of bodies which increasingly disappoint us with their nonperformance the older we get.

In Chapter 2 we also discussed how absurdly out of step with reality this ingrained cultural dualism actually is. Far from being two loosely connected entities, mind and body form a systemic whole. When we are intimidated by someone, our mouth goes dry, our face pales, and our heartbeat races. If we are attracted to someone, quite a different chain of bodily changes takes place. Just as the content of our thoughts directly impacts on our physiology, the reverse happens too. If we're suffering from a bad flu, our mood is also affected. A workout at the gym floods us with endorphins, making us feel more upbeat and positive. Mind and body form an ongoing, reciprocal, 24/7 dynamic. To focus on one as though it has no relationship with the other is to get only part of the story.

Instead of viewing disease from a physical perspective

alone, body–mind science looks at the way we interact with the outside world as a holistic entity. Why we suffer from disease says as much about our mental experience as it does about our physical condition—in particular, about how we deal with stress.

THE ROLE OF STRESS

To explain this clearly, we need to recognize the role in daily life played by the autonomic nervous system. This system is the controller of the so-called "fight–flight response," the survival mechanism inherited from our caveman ancestors. At times of stress, the fight–flight response is automatically triggered. Blood flow is diverted from the digestive system to voluntary muscles, such as in the arms and legs, where it is acutely needed. Your heart starts pumping, the energy-giving glucose level in your blood shoots up, and your senses go on red alert. In support, the endocrine system kicks in, pumping adrenalin and noradrenalin through your body to make you more alert and aggressive, while dramatically slowing production of endorphins, nitric oxide, and immune system hormones.

Once the danger has passed, the opposite reaction is triggered—a slowing heart rate, lower glucose levels, and blood directed back to the digestive system, plus hormone production which favors the immune response over fight–flight hormones. The fight–flight response was necessary to our survival in times when we were out hunting or under attack from rival tribes. There would be a set-piece event, resolved one way or another, and if we survived, life would go back to normal.

Fast forward to contemporary times and while the stress we encounter in everyday life is altogether different, our physiological response is much the same. Our reaction may be triggered by a large number of stresses—bumper-to-bumper traffic, demanding work colleagues, bosses or shareholders, challenging deadlines or production targets, faulty technology, rebellious children, fractious personal lives, and so on.

The problem is that these stresses are not set-piece events which we deal with, then move on. Instead, they're a constant feature of our lives. Our fight–flight mechanism is continually being called to action, but rarely relaxed. Many of us have an almost permanent baseline of low- to medium-level stress. In physical terms this has many serious consequences. In particular, our cardiovascular systems are repeatedly under assault from chronically raised blood pressure, and our immune systems are chronically run down.

Is it any surprise that stress-related conditions like heart disease and cancer are by far the biggest cause of death in our society? Or that infertility, gastrointestinal disorders, chronic pain, or chronic fatigue are such a pervasive part of our social landscape?

The impact of stress isn't just a matter of infrequent spikes from which we quickly bounce back, but rather an ongoing feature of the way we live. Disease, from a body–mind perspective, is caused by dis-ease: events in the external world which we experience as stressful, and to which our bodies respond in a particular way.

As Ian Gawler writes in his extremely valuable book *You Can Conquer Cancer*: "Virtually all cancer patients I have asked recognize that stress was a major factor in the development of their disease . . . In about 95 percent of patients asked, this involved one particularly severe stress experience precipitating a drastic drop in their well being. The stressful event occurred long before their cancer was diagnosed, but its untoward effect continued."

How meditation promotes healing

With some understanding about why we suffer from illness— in summary, the psychophysical impact of stress—we can see the value of creating the opposite body–mind conditions. Which is what meditation does. In Chapters 2 and 3 we have already seen the value of meditation as a preventative measure. Its contribution to healing is based on the same principles: that the body balances, regulates, and heals itself—so long as we provide it with the right conditions.

The flow chart below shows the role of stress in health and disease—and how meditation can help restore our body's natural biochemical balance.

The process described by this flow chart is really quite a simple one. By meditating we can significantly reduce our stress levels, so that our immune system works properly. This may seem almost too easy. But the impact is very powerful. To use the very well documented case of Ian Gawler himself, in January 1975 his right leg was amputated because of bone cancer. While the cancer didn't appear to exist anywhere else in his body, he was told that only five percent of patients survived more than five years after such an operation.

The role of STRESS in health and disease

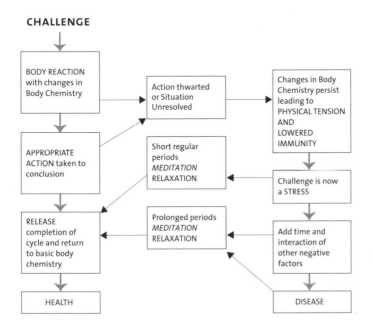

Source: Gawler 1984, p. 24

Secondary cancer did reappear in November of that same year, and by the following March his specialist thought he had no more than two weeks to live. His subsequent treatment included a range of conventional treatments—but importantly he added his own regimen of meditation, positive thinking, and a special diet. By June 1978, Ian was declared free of all active cancer, and since then he has established and managed the Gawler Foundation in Melbourne, Australia, which has helped many thousands of people fight and survive cancer by following the same highly effective regimen of meditation, positive thinking, and diet.

Is meditation being suggested as an alternative to the very best medical treatments you can get? Not at all. Instead, it is powerfully complementary. By restoring the balance of our body–mind system, meditation helps us fight disease, cope with the often toxic side effects of treatment, and maintain a more resilient and positive mental attitude.

What's more, meditation is not the only complementary practice providing enormous benefits. The support of loved ones and a formal support group, a comprehensive review of diet, and the application of positive thinking—for which mindfulness is such a great support—are other very important factors outlined in *You Can Conquer Cancer*.

Dharma Singh Khalsa, M.D., and Cameron Stauth in their illuminating book *Meditation as Medicine* refer to how meditation provides the ideal condition for healing to occur. One particular observation really struck me: "One of my patients once remarked to me that the attitude of meditation—devoid of self-criticism and judgement about others—is really one of love. Thus, in a real sense, love heals."

THE BENEFITS OF MEDITATION

Let's summarize the benefits of meditation to the healing process. I recommend that you regularly review these benefits and become thoroughly familiar with them, to support your meditation practice.

Quality of life

Significant research, including formal studies by David Spiegel and later Professor F.I. Fawzy, and overwhelming anecdotal evidence, shows that the quality of life of patients who take part in support groups, which include learning practices such as meditation and self-hypnosis, is significantly better than those who do not. Meditation helps manage pain, deal with unpleasant treatment side effects, reduce tension and blood pressure measurements, boost our immune function, and support the production of hormones such as endorphins and DHEA which have a vital role to play in helping us feel robust and live longer.

Quantity of life

The same research showed that meditation extends our life-span and improves our chances of full recovery. David Spiegel's research among women with secondary breast cancer showed that survival time was doubled. Professor Fawzy's research among melanoma patients showed significantly fewer recurrences and deaths.

To quote Ian Gawler on the work of his foundation among cancer patients: "I have seen many people now recover from very difficult medical situations. The wealth of evidence coming from the so-called 'anecdotes' of people experiencing remarkable recoveries is overwhelming. Medical research confirms the possibilities. It is possible to recover from cancer. It *is* possible."

Interestingly, one such patient was a nurse who, because of her experience in oncology wards, didn't believe that complete personal recovery was possible, but was aiming simply at extending her life somewhat by meditation and other methods. Yet when she went for a scan to check on the size of the tumor on her liver, there was no sign of it at all. "I couldn't believe it—no one else could—but there was no evidence of progressive carcinoma."

Emotional benefits

The process of diagnosis is one that is very often fraught with fear and stress. Between the time that serious illness is suspected and when it is diagnosed can be such a roller coaster of anxiety and emotion that even confirmation of our worst fears can sometimes come as a relief. But the knowledge that we have a serious illness in itself creates stress. If we persistently worry about how we and our loved ones are going to cope, whether we'll make a full recovery or if our life will be cut short, these fears only add to the stress we're under, making us feel even more anxious, tired, and overwhelmed.

Meditation helps us lift the lid off the pressure cooker. By focusing on the only thing that actually exists, this moment, here and now, we can create space and engender a state of peacefulness. If we're able to integrate meditation into our daily life through practices like spot meditation and mindfulness, we can enhance this openness and tranquility still further. If one effect of our illness is to kick-start our meditation practice, at least we will have derived one significant benefit from an otherwise unpleasant experience.

INTERPERSONAL BENEFITS

Most of us have been through the experience of a friend, relative, or colleague telling us they have been diagnosed with a serious illness. It can sometimes be an awkward experience and a source of tension in a relationship, especially if the person concerned discourages us from asking about their condition as though it's somehow embarrassing or a subject of the utmost privacy. If we are the person diagnosed, we may feel we have been a friend, businessperson, or son-in-law before the discovery of the disease, but afterwards feel we are, say, a cancer patient first and foremost. But the way that others respond to us is a very strong reflection of the way we ourselves communicate. Meditation not only helps relieve the stress we feel about having a disease; in helping our self-acceptance it also puts other people at ease, encouraging them to feel more open and compassionate in their attitude.

Two friends of mine have been diagnosed with cancer in recent years and have reacted in opposite ways. One was so open about the experience that she started a blog to keep in touch with friends all over the world. The other closed down all communication, to the extent of getting his wife to make and receive all phone calls so that he could avoid direct contact. My blogging friend kept expressing her amazement and gratitude at the level of concern and support she received, often from the least expected quarters. Gifts would turn up unexpectedly on her doorstep from the other side of the world, reminding her, sometimes in the moments she needed it most, that she continued to be in other people's thoughts. There's no doubt that both the practical suggestions, as well as the good wishes, helped her through some of the darkest periods of her treatment.

By contrast, I have no idea how my other friend has dealt with his illness, or what stage of recovery he is at. We have spoken on a few occasions about work and family life, but I haven't been able to offer any support or suggestions.

The fight against a serious illness can be likened to a journey, and there may be times in that journey when a person wants to withdraw from the world, retreat from all contact—a response which may have great value. But it's also important for people to know that it's okay to talk about their illness and to ask for help. In fact, there may be friends and loved ones wanting to provide exactly that. When we meditate, we become better at managing stress and living in the moment, making it easier to express what we are going through, and be more open to the support and friendship of others.

THE BENEFIT OF MEANING

Victor Frankl, one of the most important psychiatrists of the twentieth century and an Auschwitz survivor, saw firsthand that even in the most painful and dehumanized situations people could discover meaning, and that those with the strongest sense of purpose and meaning were the most likely to survive. People with a serious illness are often very serious about meditating. Nothing concentrates the mind like the knowledge that life is precious, potentially very short, and that this session, now, really counts. Bernice Grocke explains her meaning for living in Ian Gawler's book *Inspiring People*: "I kept telling myself how much I was needed. My husband and children need me and my grandchildren will need me."

While the motivation to meditate may be overwhelmingly to help achieve full recovery, the reality is that meditation is a holistic experience. We cannot access only some of the benefits of meditating and not others. Yes, we will enjoy the extraordinary physical benefits that flow from enabling our body to heal itself. But we will also experience ourselves in a way that's extraordinary. We may well achieve insights about our own nature and the nature of the broader reality in which we live. We may surprise ourselves with a sense of interconnectedness and transcendence. In short, we may uncover a sense of meaning in our lives which we didn't self-consciously set out to find.

This kind of revelation is by no means uncommon when seriously ill people meditate (or, indeed, when perfectly well people do so as well). On emerging at the other end, many express a sense of appreciation that their sickness forced them down a path which yielded the most unexpected benefits. Such is their gratitude that some wish the whole world could go through the same truly life-changing experience!

Some years ago a close friend of mine faced death and blindness, arising not from illness but from being injured in war. Having made a full physical recovery, with the exception of recurring eye problems, he has no doubt at all that facing his own apparently imminent death was the best thing that ever happened to him. He is now so much more relaxed and easygoing. And he doesn't take a day of his life for granted.

The final chapter of this book discusses the transformational quality of meditation in more detail, describing why it happens and how it feels. Among the many benefits of meditation, this can be the most life-changing of all.

HEALING MEDITATION TECHNIQUES

The techniques we use for healing are much the same as those already described in this book, adapted to suit our particular needs. If you haven't already done so, I'd recommend you read Chapters 4 and 5, which describe the basics of how to meditate, and provide a number of alternative techniques. How do you tailor these techniques to suit you?

DEVELOP AN INSPIRING MOTIVATION

This will be the affirmation you repeat at the beginning and end of every formal meditation session. Hopefully, you will also repeat it frequently during the day, when practicing spot meditation and mindfulness. It will be your own private affirmation, so it needs to be something that really inspires you. It's worth spending some time working out your motivation, using the guidelines already provided. By way of example, you may find the following suggestion useful or wish to personalize it further:

> By the practice of this meditation
> My whole body is vibrant with robust good health;
> My life is richly imbued with happiness and purpose
> For the sake of my family, friends, and all living beings.

FIND WHICH MEDITATION TECHNIQUE SUITS YOU BEST

Of the methods outlined in Chapters 4 and 5, there are three which lend themselves directly to healing. These are:

- Breath-based meditations
- Visualizations
- Body scanning.

Breath-based meditations

The following suggestions apply both to breath counting as well as to nine-cycle breath meditations, both of which are particularly helpful in healing. To begin with, if you are not physically able to sit on a cushion—for example, if you're currently in bed—breath-based meditations are still very useful because the object of the meditation—the breath—is so easy to find, and provides such a strong, natural focus to slow down your metabolism and create inner peace. Once you have read the core instructions on the two breath-based meditations, you may wish to consider tailoring them to suit your particular healing needs in the following ways.

- Instead of focusing your attention "like a sentry at the gate" of your nostrils, focus instead on the sensation of the breath in your lungs and abdomen as you inhale and exhale. Once you've repeated a number of breaths, and your breathing has naturally slowed, now imagine that your breath has an extraordinary healing quality. You may also want to imagine that it is colored white, a powerful purification color, or deep blue, a universal color of healing. With each in-breath, imagine you are drawing in the most powerful therapy ever created, that the colored light containing immensely potent properties is entering not only your lungs, but radiating throughout your whole body, instantly cleansing and purifying your system, getting rid of all disease or potential disease.

- You can be very specific about this if you like. For example, you may like to imagine the light radiating particularly to your heart, lungs, brain, bowel, or whichever organs are causing you concern. If you have recently suffered from a heart attack, you may find it useful to become thoroughly familiar with the human heart by studying photographs and diagrams so that when you practice this form of breathing/visualization, you can imagine exactly how the healing light fills and repairs the once-damaged blood vessels around the heart.

- In addition to breathing in colored light, you can also visualize breathing out negativity, disease, and impurity in the form of red light or dark, thick smoke. Every out-breath can become a highly effective complement to each in-breath. This can also be as specific as you wish—you can focus on your whole body or on only one organ in visualizing sickness and potential sickness leaving your body with each out-breath.

  Don't feel you have to include this aspect of a colored-light visualization immediately. You may wish to spend a few sessions focusing on getting the in-breath settled before working up to include out-breath visualizations as well.

- During the course of each session, work on increasing the vividness of the experience and the light. Do everything you can to make this a credible, believable exercise. If you want to add imagined scents or sounds, by all means do so. Remember that the brain doesn't always differentiate between what's real and what's imagined, and that by conducting this meditation you are harnessing the immense capabilities of the pharmaceutical factory in your own body. By harnessing a visualization to the breath you are creating a highly effective "pump action" treatment to be used both in formal sessions, as well as informally whenever you wish.

Visualizations

The cocoon visualization described in Chapter 5 is an ideal meditation for healing. As suggested, by imagining yourself in the middle of a cocoon of healing blue light, and drawing this light into yourself during the course of the session, you can access powerful healing qualities.

- A variation of this visualization is to imagine the healing light driving all the sickness and negativity out through the pores and orifices of your lower body. Some Tibetan Buddhist meditations take this a step further and imagine negativities in the form of insects and other bugs, as well as dark liquid, leaving the body and disappearing into the ground.
- The variations described above for breathing meditations apply equally here. Feel free to be as broad or as specific as you want, and really work at making this the most powerful experience you can.
- If it helps, by all means use a powerful figure to emanate the light. This may be the founder of a world religion, like Jesus or Buddha, or a figure for whom you feel particular devotion or respect, like Mother Theresa, John Paul II, the Dalai

Lama, or some other figure of positive energy to whom you feel particularly connected. If you have a natural sense that this being would want you to be healed, quickly and completely, harness this belief in your meditation, turning your motivation into a form of prayer.

Body scanning

Body scanning is a particularly useful meditation practice, both in its own right and also as a form of warm-up before commencing breath-based meditation or visualization. Because you systematically work through your body from head to toe, by the time you complete this exercise you should be a lot more physically relaxed than before. With practice, you can learn to vary the speed at which you carry out this meditation, so that you can vary it from a shorter, preparatory exercise to a much longer meditation in its own right.

- I would recommend the variation of clenching and releasing each muscle group, as far as possible, as you work through the body. This enhances awareness of your physical self in a way that is particularly useful given that the focus of your meditation is on healing.
- The practice of body scanning may also be helpful if you're in bed, and/or before going to sleep, as a way of reducing mental agitation and inducing relaxation.
- Once you've completed your scan, an enjoyable addition, when you've induced a relaxed response, is to imagine you are floating in a pool of warm syrup (if you're feeling overheated, make that cool syrup). If you'd like to go to sleep at

this point, imagine your body sinking through the syrup, lower and lower, as you get heavier and heavier, sleepier and sleepier . . .

MAKING HEALING MEDITATION PART OF EVERYDAY LIFE

During the course of his work with literally thousands of seriously ill people, Ian Gawler maintains that quality of life is significantly improved by two or three sessions each lasting twenty minutes, while to make an impact on quantity of life requires three daily hour-long sessions. However, to attempt even a single hour-long session, if you've never meditated in your life before, is almost guaranteed to set yourself up for failure—much better to have three enjoyable ten-minute sessions and build your way up from there, step by step.

Three hours of meditation a day may seem like an unreasonable demand. But as one cancer sufferer explains, "I went from French champagne and caviar to fruit juice and carrots! It was an effort, but given the motivation it was easy." When we know or have met people who've been through what we have, and successfully come out the other end, this gives us the confidence to use the same tools they did, to find the same commitment.

While formal sessions provide the foundation of our practice, no matter how disciplined it is we should also try to integrate meditative experience into our off-cushion reality. The advice given in Chapter 6 certainly applies here, in particular finding opportunities to practice spot meditation and mindfulness.

For healing purposes, visits to the toilet are ideal opportunities to practice healing meditation. After mentally reciting your motivation, imagine being suffused with healing blue light, which drives all sickness and life-shortening disease out through the lower orifices. Body and mind become one.

Any form of cleaning, be it showering, dishwashing, brushing teeth, sweeping the veranda, or cleaning the car—if you're at a stage in your recovery where you're up to it—can be transformed into an exercise in purification, as you imagine your external actions reflecting what's happening at an inner level. We can imagine any form of eating and especially drinking as being the same as ingesting the most powerful active healing components available. We can drink a cup of tea as a cup of tea, or imagine that it's the most potent chemotherapy ever invented. Which is the more likely to benefit us?

A friend of mine who is recovering from lung cancer told me how helpful it has been for her to feel she's doing something positive to promote her own healing through the journey to recovery. In the difficult weeks between the diagnosis of her illness and surgery to remove a lung, she decided she was going to become as fit as she possibly could, going for long, brisk walks every day, including climbing sessions up and down Jacob's Ladder, a huge tower of stairs used by serious fitness fanatics and by trainee mountaineers with rucksacks full of bricks. Nobody told her to do this. Her doctor didn't prescribe it. But she was told afterwards that her high level of fitness had been a great advantage for her postsurgical recovery.

"BEYOND MEDICAL HELP"

I'd like to end this chapter with one of the many uplifting stories from *Inspiring People*—of someone who, like many of the people profiled, was considered to be beyond medical help. Jean Fraser is a grandmother who, after a series of worsening medical problems, found herself in hospital undergoing a CAT scan. The results could not have been more serious. The surface of her pancreas was a mass of bumps, and she had cancer that was so far advanced she was told there was nothing that could be done to save her. She should go home and only return when she started turning yellow.

This occurred one January. Within a short while, Jean was attending a support group at the Gawler Foundation, had radically changed her diet to cut out salt, sugar, and meat, and had begun to meditate for two hours a day. Paradoxically, she began to feel in better physical shape than she had for years.

That northern-hemisphere summer, she and her husband decided to go to New York to visit their son and his family, enjoying a relaxing holiday together. On their return, Jean decided to go to see her doctor for a check-up. He was astonished when he looked at her card and saw what her diagnosis had been nine months earlier—he'd obviously expected her condition to have seriously deteriorated well before then. After feeling her tummy, and finding no evidence of any bumps, he then ordered X rays, which showed nothing. He was so mystified that he rechecked the original biopsy to confirm that cancer had most certainly been present in her pancreas.

Jean called her brother, a consulting physician, who recommended a second opinion and CAT scan. This more detailed scan showed that her pancreas was perfectly normal and healthy.

I have highlighted this story not as a claim for the powers of meditation alone, because Jean also made significant changes to her diet and attended a support group. But it's important to remember that along with the authority and expertise of people in white coats, there is another paradigm, one in which meditation, together with other complementary practices, has an important part to play. We shouldn't underestimate the power we can access in this paradigm, or its possibilities for personal transformation. Because of it, there are many, many people living among us today who were once considered "beyond medical help."

CHAPTER NINE

Troubleshooting

WE DON'T UNDERSTAND THE OPERATIONS OF OUR MIND AND HENCE
WE DON'T OPERATE THEM VERY WELL.
CHARLES TART, PSYCHOLOGIST

I HOPE TO have answered any questions that readers may
have about the practicalities of meditation (such as how to
cope with agitation or drowsiness) in the main body of this
book. There are, nevertheless, some higher-level questions
which don't fit neatly into any of the previous chapters. Just
as most software packages today come with a troubleshooting
guide, it seems only right that meditation, the ultimate self-
improvement program, should come with a troubleshooting
chapter too.

Q. Can meditation be bad for some people, if not dangerous?
I've heard of people going crazy on silent meditation retreats,
or that meditation has made their depression even worse.
A. I've also heard these stories and I'm quite sure they're true.
I don't believe that meditation is bad for anyone, but the *inap-
propriate* use of meditation certainly could be. For someone
with very little experience of meditation to suddenly attempt
a retreat is a bit like an ordinary person wanting to take up

athletics and starting by attempting to train with the national Olympic squad.

An important emphasis of this book is to begin practice with short, enjoyable sessions before building up—that is, taking baby steps. If you stick with this and, as also recommended, find a meditation teacher/class, there's no reason you shouldn't find meditation the most life-enhancing thing you've ever done.

Q. What is the difference between hypnosis and meditation?

A. While there may appear to be certain similarities, there are a number of significant differences. First, we've seen that there are certain physical and psychological markers that are characteristic of a meditative state. But there is no psychophysical state which is characteristic of hypnosis. Yes, a person may be deeply relaxed, but he or she could just as easily be perspiring and have a racing heartbeat if that is the suggestion of the hypnotist. Second, in a meditative state we strive to be completely mindful of the object of meditation through the application of conscious will. But in a hypnotized or trance state there is no attempt to be mindful or to apply our conscious will. In fact we give the hypnotist authority to guide our thoughts and mental behavior. Hypnosis can be an extremely powerful tool for change, especially in dealing with phobias and self-destructive habits, but it is a different process from meditation.

Q. Is there a short cut? Achieving perfect concentration seems to take years to achieve, but I've seen advertisements saying that you can meditate deeper than a Zen monk just by listening to CDs.

A. There's no short cut that I've found. But as I hope this book has shown, our individual meditative journeys can be as important as reaching the destination. Every time I see a "short cut" advertised, I follow up on it. I'm truly open to ideas. But invariably I've discovered people selling hypnosis or trance induction instead of meditative concentration. And while going into a trance state can be very relaxing and pleasurable, it is quite different from meditation (see the preceding question).

Q. Is meditation anti-intellectual?

A. When we are engaged in meditation, we deliberately avoid all discursive thought, including intellectual abstraction. But this practice is complementary to intellectual activity, rather than opposed to it. One's understanding of concepts is immeasurably deepened when explored through meditation. We need look no further than Tibetan Buddhism to see how an extremely elaborate philosophical system is supported by the practice of meditation. Meditation provides us with a different pathway to knowledge than the intellectual, as described in the final chapter of this book. But intellectual and direct, or non-conceptual, understanding are mutually supportive.

Q. What are the similarities and differences between meditation, Tai Chi, and yoga?

A. Tai Chi, yoga, and meditation practices like breath counting or walking meditation all seek to develop mindfulness of body. Body and mind are brought together in union—which is what the word "yoga" refers to. In this sense one might see Tai Chi and yoga as being types of meditation. Tai Chi and yoga also place great importance on the breath and flow of energy through a subtle body comprising chakras and energy channels—a model shared by some Buddhist meditations. While the practice of all three disciplines would be highly complementary, in general it's fair to say that yoga and Tai Chi focus more on mindfulness of body while many meditation practices place more emphasis on mindfulness of mind, or objects of mind such as mantra and visualization.

Q. I've read of people meditating to increase their wealth and success—"chanting for a Porsche." Does this work?

A. You will not be surprised to learn that I have looked into this very closely. After all, why go to the trouble of having to go out every day to earn money if you can spend just an hour rattling off magical mantras before scheduling your appointment at the local Porsche dealership? In the section on visualization (Chapter 5) I describe the power of suggestion, and how we can help achieve a desired outcome—which may include owning a Porsche—if we self-consciously set ourselves a goal, regularly remind ourselves of this goal when in a relaxed state, and visualize ourselves as the recipients of wealth, success, and, yes, even a Porsche Carrera. At levels both conscious and beneath our conscious awareness, this technique can help us notice opportunities, behave in a goal-fulfilling way, and reinforce behaviors which lead to us achieving our desired outcome. But is magic involved? Is there an external energy we can invoke? Can we somehow tilt the universe in our favor? Until proper experiments are undertaken we won't really know for sure.

It is also worth recalling the difference between pleasure and happiness (Chapter 3). Our main goal as meditators is to cultivate an enduring state of inner happiness rather than to strive for the short-lived pleasure we enjoy from rearranging our external conditions.

Q. Meditation is a part of the world's major religious traditions, but this book doesn't mention God, the divine, the soul, or spirit even once. Why is that?

A. We don't need to accept any particular belief system to benefit from meditation. What I've attempted is to provide a starter kit for people wanting to know how to meditate, as well as to outline the pretty amazing physical and psychological benefits of meditative practices. Some readers may place religion at the very heart of their lives. Others may feel completely alienated by traditional religion. The reason why meditation can benefit both groups is because it operates at a level different from that concerned with thought, belief, or emotion. When we meditate we actively abandon discursive mental activity, regarding it as akin to passing clouds when the focus of our concentration is on the sky. Paradoxically, the result of this nonconceptual experience is to make us realize the complete unimportance of conceptual elaborations, including belief systems, just as we recognize the true nature of the consciousness we share with other sentient beings.

From such a vantage, we come to view belief systems for what they are—different ladders leading to the same understanding—but it is the understanding that is important, not the ladders.

Q. Seeing that meditation delivers such amazing physiological and psychological benefits, why don't a lot more people do it?

A. Because it is hard work and requires self-discipline. Also because even though meditation is now much more mainstream than it was even a few decades ago, we have still not reached the point of critical mass where it's considered just as normal to go to meditation class as it is to go to the gym. But hopefully we are getting there.

Q. You sometimes hear people say, "I go for a walk in the morning/swim in the sea/work in my vegetable patch—that's my meditation." Will these activities cause the same positive effects as described earlier?

A. The application of mindfulness to most activities will yield very positive results. So if the walker, swimmer, or gardener enjoys pure presence for much of the time they're embarked on that activity, it could be described as meditation. That said, we still need to apply mindfulness and awareness. We still need to guard against agitation. Without these tools, the quality of the meditation may not be very good, and what we end up with is enjoyable recreation, which may be useful for stress relief, but is not really meditation. When we start out, and until we've mastered mindfulness, it's much easier to learn to meditate sitting down, and cut off from external stimuli, so that we only have one set of distractions—internal distractions—to contend with.

CHAPTER 10

A Bigger Picture

REALITY IS AN ILLUSION, ALBEIT A PERSISTENT ONE.
ALBERT EINSTEIN (ATTRIBUTED)

S INCE ANCIENT times, the wisdom of self-knowledge has been held above all other. Some believe that it is the real purpose of our life's journey. In ancient Greece, when seekers visited the Temple at Delphi to ask what the future held, they would see etched above the door the words which gave the implicit answer to their question: "Know thyself." Later, Socrates identified this as the pinnacle of human wisdom, and became famous for his words "The unexamined life is not worth living."

But what is really meant by "Know thyself"? When I first heard the phrase I used to puzzle over what it suggested. Applying it personally, I wondered if there was really that much to know. After all, the facts of my life, like most people's, are easily summarized. I have some awareness of my own strengths and failings. In the past I've undertaken psychometric testing and a personality assessment. What else is there to know?

As it happens, it is in this area of self-knowledge that the benefits of meditation are, for me, the most significant. For as I've come to discover, the practice of meditation provides an inner pathway—in a sense a road less travelled—which I know

I will continue to follow until at least the end of this particular lifetime.

In trying to explain why, the best starting point is probably the definition of "knowledge." Generally speaking, we think of knowledge as a linear, single-dimensional thing. A high school graduate may have a certain level of knowledge about human biology. Seven years later, graduating from medical school, she will know much more. We take our faulty car to the garage because we trust that the mechanic has greater knowledge than ourselves to identify and repair the problem. And so on.

But I don't believe this is the kind of knowledge referred to in the phrase "Know thyself." This form of knowledge, involving the accumulation and assimilation of information, is essentially intellectual. And there are other forms of knowledge, which, in this context, are of far greater value. Specifically, these are conceptual and nonconceptual knowledge. The differences between intellectual, conceptual, and nonconceptual knowledge are perhaps best described by an illustration.

Suppose we came across a man from a landlocked country who had never been to the sea, but who wanted to know what it was like. For the purposes of this example, we'll also assume he'd never seen the sea on TV or at the movies either. One way to explain the sea would be to sit him down and tell him all about the chemistry of the saline environment, the biology of the sea—flora and fauna—as well as the physics of the ocean, with the effects of the wind and gravity on the waves and tides. After such a lesson, the man would have an *intellectual* knowledge of the sea. If any of his fellow landlocked friends had the temerity to suggest that the sea was brown in color, or that cattle grazed contentedly on the ocean bed, he could soon set them straight. But despite this intellectual knowledge, would he really have very much idea of what the sea was really like, or would it still be largely an intellectual abstraction to him?

A different way to deal with his request would be to suggest he visualize the biggest lake he'd ever seen, and then imagine the lake extending all the way to the horizon. We could describe waves forming and breaking, water rushing up a beach to where he is standing in his imagination, the smell of ozone, and the calls of seagulls overhead. Using all the sense perceptions available, we could encourage him to build up an image as vivid as possible so that he developed a good *conceptual* knowledge of the sea.

His experience would naturally depend on the power of his imagination. However, his conceptual knowledge would be quite different from the intellectual approach. He would experience a similitude of the sea far more like the real thing. But when he opened his eyes, his conceptual vision of the sea would disappear, and he'd once again find himself in landlocked reality.

The best way, by far, to satisfy his curiosity, would be to put him on a plane, fly him to the nearest coastal resort, and book him into a beachside chalet for two weeks. By the end of his stay he would know exactly what the sea is like, and his knowledge would be direct and first hand: *nonconceptual.*

It's easy to see the advantages of nonconceptual knowledge over alternative approaches. Both intellectual and conceptual knowledge are dependent on other people and therefore unreliable. What if, a short time after our biology, chemistry, and physics lesson, someone else turned up and refuted our description of the sea, saying it was deeply flawed? We were putting him on with our descriptions of dolphins, whales, and fish—the sea is so salty that there's no life in it at all. The fact that this new expert lived near the Dead Sea, and was therefore perfectly correct in terms of his own limited experience, only underlines the serious limitations of intellectual knowledge, which is necessarily restrictive and subject to instant revision.

Applying these three ways of knowing things to the injunction "Know thyself," we make the unsettling discovery that most of what we take to be self-knowledge tends to be at the intellectual level. We can, if prompted, rattle off our biographies, our work and family lives, our likes and dislikes, our fears and aspirations. We might describe our personal quirks, hobbies, and prejudices. But how meaningful is any of that information? Just because we can give a comprehensive factual account of the entity labelled "me," "myself," or "I," like the man with the intellectual knowledge of the sea, do we really have very much idea what this "I" is really like?

This may seem a shocking, if not outrageous, idea. But let's be honest about where all these facts and beliefs about "me" came from in the first place. Did we discover them for ourselves, or did we get them secondhand? At a very young age, when we overheard Dad telling someone that we couldn't hit a ball to save our lives, did that start the beginning of a self-fulfilling idea that we're hopeless in sports? When the math teacher we secretly admired congratulated us on our quadratic equations, did this spur us on to tackle more advanced calculations with greater confidence?

And how firmly held are these ideas about ourselves? By the time we reach middle age, most of us have experienced enough ups and downs in our personal, marital, or professional lives to know how profoundly a turn of events can change long-held ideas about who we are and what's important to us. Even without major personal earthquakes, little by little our priorities and attitudes naturally shift as we negotiate our way through different life stages.

It has become a cliché that the erstwhile bad boys of art and pop over time become members of the very establishment they once rebelled against. Diehard socialists become the most venal capitalists. Carnivores become vegetarians—and back again. Pillars of society decamp to sunny, coastal resorts with their executive assistants.

And what's going on when we say we believe certain things, then behave in a completely contradictory way? We say we want to lose weight, but don't stop stuffing our faces with comfort food. We claim that world peace is important, but are always giving our spouse, kids, and colleagues a hard time. Do our actions negate our sincerity, or is there some other explanation for our behavior?

What I've tried to do in these few paragraphs—and it would be easy to go on—is simply to illustrate how it's possible for us to have the most detailed and coherent ideas about who we are, but like all intellectual abstractions, these beliefs may not be very relevant, accurate, or could be subject to abrupt change. How much value do they really have?

Meditation provides an entirely different approach. Instead of intellectual elaborations, it provides us with the means of knowing ourselves both conceptually and, ultimately, nonconceptually. Just as a whole load of facts and figures about the sea is not the sea, so too all the thoughts I have about me are not me. The label is not the product. If I really want to know me, I have to clear my mind of all conceptions, interruptions, and distractions and find out what's really there. This is why when we sit on our cushions and focus our minds on just one thing, we are doing something unique that goes against all our usual mental behavior. We are allowing our minds to settle.

An illustration of this point which I particularly like is the jar of swirling grey storm water. Allow it to rest for half an hour and the sediment falls to the bottom, providing perfect clarity. In much the same way, when we consciously focus our minds in meditation, if we are able to free ourselves from all the usual discursive thinking, we can start to see ourselves for who and what we really are.

Or as Dr. Kabat-Zinn puts it, "Dwelling in stillness and looking inward for some part of each day, we touch what is most real and reliable in ourselves and most easily overlooked and undeveloped. When we can be centered in ourselves, even for brief periods of time in the face of the pull of the outer world, not having to look elsewhere for something to fill us up or make us happy, we can be at home wherever we find ourselves, at peace with things as they are, moment by moment."

Of course the best way to encounter ourselves is directly, or nonconceptually, in a state of deep meditative equipoise. But this takes a lot of practice. In our early years of meditation most of us can only hope to catch brief glimpses of our true state of being before, like clouds concealing a mountain peak, agitation or dullness get in the way. Which is why we need to continue in our efforts, inspired by a conceptual account of our ultimate nature. Just as you might encourage the landlocked man to create a vivid image of what the sea may be like, so too when you start to meditate it helps to imagine how it might be if your mind were undistracted.

Some of the inspiration for what we are trying to experience nonconceptually tells us that our ultimate nature is like a cloudless sky: boundless, perfectly clear, undisturbed by any form of agitation. It is a state of peacefulness and bliss, paradoxically both empty of anything as well as offering the potential for everything—because all things begin with thought. This "open field" state is one in which our usually tightly held sense of "me-ness" dissolves into a more panoramic vista that things simply are, without subject or object, self or other. To me, even just to catch a glimpse of this "self" is the most important benefit of meditation. I know of no other practice which has the potential to transform my understanding of who, or what, I am—and, by contrast, what I am not.

For like the once landlocked man emerging from the waves onto the beach at the end of his first day in the sea, once we have experienced the reality of who we are at a direct, nonconceptual level, no one can take the experience away from us. And we can never go back to believing ourselves to be merely a collection of intellectual beliefs and abstractions. We know that all that stuff is merely transient, ever-changing—the clouds rather than the sky.

The self with its personal quirks, hobbies, and prejudices is not the subject of the edict "Know thyself." Rather it is the self that is subject to no boundaries, that experiences the unity of all, that abides in a state of blissful transcendence, which it is our life's true purpose to discover.

References

Chapter 2 The Physical Benefits of Meditation

M. Murphy and S. Donovan, *The Physical and Psychological Effects of Meditation*, Institute of Noetic Sciences, <www.noetic.org>, accessed 15 October 2007.

Mind/Body Medical Institute/Benson-Henry Institute for Mind Body Medicine, <www.mbmi.org>, accessed 19 October 2007.

Center for Mindfulness in Medicine, Health Care, and Society, University of Massachusetts, <www.umassmed.edu>, accessed 19 October 2007.

Clinical trial of 106 patients: M. Paul-Labrador et al., "Effects of a Randomized Controlled Trial of Transcendental Meditation on Components of the Metabolic Syndrome in Subjects with Coronary Heart Disease," *Archives of Internal Medicine* 166 (2006): 1218–24.

Clinical trial of heart disease patients who practiced meditation for eight months: J. W. Zamarra et al., "Usefulness of the transcendental meditation program in the treatment of patients with coronary artery disease," *American Journal of Cardiology* 77(10) [1996]: 867–70.

Clinical trial among elderly subjects: R. H. Schneider et al., "Trial of stress reduction for hypertension in older African Americans. II. Sex and risk subgroup analysis," *Hypertension* 28(20) [1996]: 228–37.

Research by R. K. Wallace: "Physiological Effects of Transcendental Meditation," *Science* 167 (1970): 1751–4.

Information on melatonin from University of Maryland Medical Center: Complementary and Alternative Medicine Index, <www.umm.edu/altmed>, accessed 19 October 2007.

Information on DHEA from studies collated by *Life Extension Magazine*, August 2001: I. Greenwell, "DHEA Anti-Aging Hormone," cover story, <www.lef.org>, accessed 19 October 2007.

R. K. Wallace, "Transcendental Meditation and Ageing," *International Journal of Neuroscience* 16 (1982): 53–8.

C. N. Alexander et al., "Transcendental Meditation, mindfulness, and longevity: An experimental study with the elderly," *Journal of Personality and Social Psychology* 57(6) [1989]: 950–64.

R. K. Wallace, J. Silver, P. J. Mills et al., "Systolic Blood Pressure and Long-Term Practice of the Transcendental Meditation and TM-Sidhi Program: Effects of TM on Systolic Blood Pressure," *Psychosomatic Medicine* 45(1) [1983]: 41–6.

Chapter 3 The Psychological Benefits of Meditation

The research conducted by Dr. Richard Davidson from the University of Wisconsin and Dr. Jon Kabat-Zinn from the University of Massachusetts is extensively covered in His Holiness the Dalai Lama and Daniel Goleman, "The Lama in the Lab," in *Destructive Emotions: How Can We Overcome Them?* (New York: Bantam Books, 2003), pp. 3–27.

Albert Ellis Institute, <www.albertellisinstitute.org>, accessed 19 October 2007.

G. Gorman, quoted on Southeastern Yearly Meeting of the Religious Society of Friends (Quakers) Meeting for Worship, <www.seym. org>, accessed 21 November 2007.

The Enlightened Sentencing Project, <http://enlightenedsentencing.org> (for judges' testimonials), accessed 19 October 2007. Dubrovnik Peace Project, <www.dubrovnik-peace-project.cro. net>, accessed 19 October 2007.

W. M. Keck Laboratory "dose response" experiments: M. Kaufman, "Meditation Gives Brain a Charge, Study Finds," *Washington Post*, 3 January 2005, p. A05.

Work by Daniel Kahneman and Daniel Gilbert referenced in C. Flora, "Happy Hour," *Psychology Today*, Jan/Feb 2005.

Dr. Michael King, interviewed by Rebecca Carmody on ABC Radio, 3 December 2004. Transcript: "New sentencing regime keeping offenders out of prison," <www.abc.net.au/stateline/wa>, accessed 19 October 2007.

Chapter 6 Seven Ways to Turbocharge Your Meditation

Eckhart Tolle, *The Power of Now: A Guide to Spiritual Enlightenment* (Novato, Calif.: New World Library, 2004).

Chapter 7 Measuring Progress

The Dalai Lama, *Words of Wisdom from the Dalai Lama*, compiled by Margaret Gee (New York: Gramercy Books, 2005), p. 49.

Chapter 8 Using Meditation to Heal

Research: D. Spiegel et al., "Effect of psychosocial treatment on survival of patients with metastatic breast cancer," *The Lancet* no. 8668 (1989): 888-91; F.I. Fawzy et al., "A structured psychiatric intervention for cancer patients. II. Changes over time in immunological measures," *Archives of General Psychiatry* 47 (1990): 729–35; F.I. Fawzy et al., "Malignant melanoma. Effects of an early structured psychiatric intervention, coping, and affective state on recurrence and survival 6 years later," *Archives of General Psychiatry* 50 (1993): 681-89.

Further Reading

Pema Chödrön, *The Wisdom of No Escape*. Boston: Shambhala, 1991.

Ian Gawler, ed., *Inspiring People: Stories of Remarkable Recovery and Hope from the Gawler Foundation*. Melbourne: Gawler Foundation, 1995.

Ian Gawler, *You Can Conquer Cancer*. Melbourne: Michelle Anderson Publishing, 2007.

Thich Nhat Hanh, *The Miracle of Mindfulness*. Boston: Beacon Press, 1987.

Thich Nhat Hanh, *The Heart of Understanding*. Berkeley: Parallax Press, 1988.

His Holiness the Dalai Lama, *Words of Wisdom from the Dalai Lama*, compiled by Margaret Gee. New York: Gramercy Books, 2005.

His Holiness the Dalai Lama and Howard C. Cutler, M.D., *The Art of Happiness*. New York: Riverhead Books, 1998.

His Holiness the Dalai Lama and Daniel Goleman, *Destructive Emotions: How Can We Overcome Them?* New York: Bantam Books, 2003.

Jon Kabat-Zinn, *Wherever You Go, There You Are: Mindfulness Meditation in Everyday Life*. New York: Hyperion, 2005.

Dharma Singh Khalsa and Cameron Stauth, *Meditation as Medicine*, New York: Pocket Books, 2001.

Sogyal Rinpoche, *The Tibetan Book of Living and Dying*. San Francisco: HarperSanFrancisco, 2002.